Hildegard

By

Pauline Bantel

Copyright © 2025 Pauline Bantel

ISBN: 978-1-918264-86-9

All rights reserved, including the right to reproduce this book, or portions thereof in any form. No part of this text may be reproduced, transmitted, downloaded, decompiled, reverse engineered, or stored, in any form or introduced into any information storage and retrieval system, in any form or by any means, whether electronic or mechanical without the express written permission of the author.

DEDICATION

To Hildegard's children,

her grandchildren

and her great grandchildren.

This is her story.

PREFACE

The seed to write an account of my mother-in-law's life was first planted when a WWII homework task given to my daughter required her to ask a grandparent about their wartime experiences. Her older siblings, when previously set the same assignment, had asked their maternal (English) grandparents for their reminiscences, so my youngest decided instead to talk to her paternal and German grandmother for a different perspective. Like many who have lived through a war, her grandmother had shared little to nothing with her family about those difficult years, maybe preferring to forget, so the part of her story she provided was new to us all.

Hildegard gave our daughter a never-seen-before snapshot of her younger life in Nazi Germany and, pleased with our interest, and happy for me to ask more questions, she began to relate further stories. Realising this wasn't easy for her as she struggled with the order of things, I suggested she might find it simpler to write down her memories in her own time and in her mother tongue to help the flow. I was eventually presented with several pages of her handwritten story, in German, which I translated into English with the help of Google! I now had the bare bones and after many hours of research, and interviews where I was amazed by her ability to remember so much detail, I used 'Lock Down 2020' to begin putting it all together. Despite hindrances along the way threatening to thwart completion, Hildegard's story became a labour of love as I emulated her determination to achieve a goal, against all odds.

With thanks to my family for their encouragement, to my grandchildren for proofreading help, together with their genuine interest, enthusiasm and joy, and to God for providing health and strength, I hope Hildegard's family and others will be blessed by her story of faith and courage.

NB All references regarding Germany and WWII, although as accurate and extensive as possible, are not complete and are used purely as a backdrop and explanation pertaining to Hildegard's life in Nazi Germany, and the subsequent and shocking expulsions from her homeland towards the end of the war.

Part One

1923 - 1933

Chapter 1

Upper Silesia, East Germany 1923

The story begins in the region of *Oberschlesien* (Upper Silesia), situated on the upper Oder River in Eastern Europe, incorporating Germany and Poland. Upper Silesia was hugely important economically due to its abundance of coal, iron ore, lead and zinc mines and its successful manufacturing industry. Naturally, both Germans and Poles wished to have control over the region and the ongoing tensions caused uprisings between 1919 and 1921. The final uprising had culminated in the dispute being submitted to The League of Nations, the result of which was the German-Polish Accord and the redrawing of borders. The western half of Upper Silesia was to be incorporated into Germany with the eastern half remaining as part of Poland, with neither country being happy with the outcome.

By 1923, although enjoying a time of peace after the 1914-18 World War, Germany was coming to terms with the devastation of defeat. The Treaty of Versailles, signed by the Allied Powers and Germany at the end of the war in 1919, had left the country bereft. Territories and colonies were confiscated as a means of punishment to Germany for being involved in the start of the war as well as a huge bill for reparations to France and Britain for the damage wrought on those countries. The value of the Mark had decreased rapidly causing much hardship as the population struggled to feed themselves.

Away from urban areas however, in the smaller farming communities where the inhabitants grew and reared much of their own food, life was somewhat easier due to self-sufficiency. They weren't rich but their lives continued more or less as usual.

In one such community in the West Upper Silesian region of Eastern Germany a young man, Josef Scheitza, had asked his sweetheart to marry him. Maria Kroworsch lived in a neighbouring village and they had known each other since they were young. Joseph was one of 9 children and Maria had two brothers. Family, friends and neighbours gathered to wish the couple well on their wedding day and after the celebrations, waved them off to the small rented apartment they had chosen to be their first home together. The apartment, located in the beautiful spa town of Carlsruhe (renamed Pokoj), was situated a little over 4km from Jaginne.

Josef and Maria had visited the town many times and had decided this was where they would like to live once they were married. It would be in complete contrast to the rural farmlands they had both grown up in and they were excited at the prospect. Carlsruhe boasted an ancient castle which was built and established as a hunting lodge in 1748 by Duke Charles Christian Erdmann of Wurttenberg. A settlement of white houses was built around it and from there eight streets radiated outwards to the surrounding areas like a star. Also spreading out from beyond the castle were exquisitely landscaped gardens containing numerous monuments, sculptures and statues including one of Otto von Bismarck, the first Chancellor of the German Empire in the nineteenth century. Outwards from the gardens were acres of parkland, including a picturesque boating lake, with the whole town being bordered by woodland. On public holidays beautiful music would be heard throughout the park which added to the wonderful aura of this idyllic place.

As well as various shops, there were two churches, one Protestant and one Roman Catholic. Residents were very proud of the ancient history of their town, its beauty and its 'almost royal' owners. Although the current Duke did not actually live in Carlsruhe, he would spend holidays at the castle when he would be seen driving around in his horse and carriage. His favourite pastime was to shoot deer and wild boar in the nearby woods. He and his wife would attend church on Sundays and sit in their own bespoke balcony positioned near the altar, elevated above the rest of the congregation.

Carlsruhe received the status of a spa town, thence known as *Bad* Carlsruhe (*Bad* meaning Spa). The local waters were found to have healing properties and the town attracted many tourists visiting for weekends and holidays. Pine needles in the baths of spa water were apparently effective in the healing of tuberculosis. The pine needles initially turned the skin brown, but could eventually be washed off. In those impoverished days after the Great War, the local people would marvel at the many elegantly dressed and wealthy ladies and gentlemen taking strolls or riding in horse drawn carriages around the parkland, having enjoyed the calm and relaxation of the spa. For the newly-weds it was a dream come true to actually live in this delightful town and it was a wonderful place to begin their married life.

It was in Carlsruhe, a year into their marriage on 10th October 1924, that Josef and Maria welcomed their first child, a daughter who they named Hildegard.

Two years later the couple happily announced the safe arrival of a second daughter, Margarete, a sister for Hildegard, with her name being immediately shortened to Gretel. Aware of the young family's need for more space Josef's parents, who owned a large farm in Jaginne, decided to portion off 2 acres of their land as a gift to their son and his wife.

Jaginne was a small farming community with one shop and a guest house which included a bar used for weddings and celebrations. The village comprised mainly smallholdings and larger farms with the whole being bordered by acres of deep forest. Although the decision to move away from Carlsruhe with its beautiful parkland and shops was a difficult one, the couple had to admit that they did indeed need more space now they were a family of four. The land, they realised, was an offer they could not refuse and the move would not take them too far away from the town they loved. Maria was happy that she would still be able to visit Carlsruhe and enjoy its many benefits.

In addition to this very generous gift, Maria had received a dowry from her parents on her wedding day for the purpose of purchasing a home of their own. An architect was employed to draw up plans to build a chalet bungalow on the land, leaving plenty of space to include sectioned fields and space for a few animals. Although a small child, Hildegard remembered the excitement of their new home being built. Her father's brothers were exceptionally skilled and they were more than happy to carry out the building work. Their accumulated talents ranged from bricklaying, carpentry and plumbing, meeting all essential requirements. Her father would help when he could but the long hours spent at his job at the railway station in Carlsruhe meant his time was limited.

After six months, when the building reached the halfway mark, a party was arranged and Josef and Maria prepared a feast with plenty of food and drink to celebrate with all the helpers. Paper chains were hung around the walls and a nearby tree was festooned with balloons and bunting. A happy celebration with family, friends and neighbours to reward the workers.

The day finally arrived when the family could happily move into their brand-new home. The bungalow was perfect. There were two main rooms, one a living room which included a kitchen with a stove and cupboards and a bench table. The other was a bedroom for the family to share. Each parent would share a bed with one of the children. In addition, there was a small bathroom with a tin bath which would be also used for washing the laundry. A few steps down, under the house, was a cellar, a large part of which would be used as a 'cool room', essential for food storage in preparation for the winter months.

In the roof was a large loft space which the couple planned to turn into another bedroom as their daughters grew. Due to the cold winter months removable secondary glazing was fitted to all the windows of the bungalow.

Outside there was a *Laube* (covered veranda) where the family could sit in the spring and summer. A grapevine was planted and as the years went by the family watched its progress as it spread over the veranda and stretched all around the bungalow.

Bordering onto their property, on the land belonging to Josef's parents, was a meadow full of pretty marguerite daisies which gleamed in the sunlight like a huge white pillow. It was such a spectacular sight that people out for a drive in their horsedrawn wagons or drays would stop to admire the view and many would pick a posy of flowers for themselves. There were no objections to this but Maria would quickly give anyone a piece of her mind whose horses or cart wheels were seen to be spoiling the grass verge.

Chapter 2

Germany After the Great War

In 1919 aged 30, but with no career after his hopes of becoming an artist had been dashed, a young and fiercely patriotic man named Adolf Hitler joined the 55 person German Workers Party. He had fought in The Great War, had twice been badly wounded, and was the recipient of two Iron Crosses for bravery. Like many Germans he was shocked and disappointed at his country's defeat and hated the Government for signing the armistice, blaming much of the decision-making on the Jewish contingent within the Government. He was greatly angered by the Treaty of Versailles and the debts incurred by his country when in fact many of his countrymen had also lost their lives. A further reason for his fury was the forced reduction of the military to ensure Germany kept the peace.

Within a couple of years Adolf Hitler was elected Chairman and leader of the German Workers' Party. He immediately changed the Party's name to the *Nationalsozialistische Deutsche Arbeiterpartei* (National Socialist German Workers' Party), this title being shortened to the 'Nazi Party'. He was ambitious and determined to make a difference and turn things around by taking the Nazi Party into Government. In a short time, under his leadership, the Party's membership grew to 2,000.

In his new role Hitler developed a 25-point programme to reverse Germany's economic situation should they come to power, which they were indeed working towards. The points on the programme were designed to appeal to the majority, including socialists, nationalists, racists and fascists, and would hopefully win the entire nation's support. The points firstly suggested the abolishment of the Treaty of Versailles. Other points included the suggestion that the country should be led by a single strong leader and there should be jobs and a good lifestyle for everyone. His desire was for his country's population to solely comprise people of German blood and birth, a superior Aryan race, and that Jews in particular, who he saw as 'subhuman', along with Communists, should be exiled. His aim was to create a strong Germany that was self-sufficient and which would excel as a successful nation to be reckoned with. He also saw the need for more *Lebenstraum* (living space) to enable the German nation to expand.

The state of the economy continued to go from bad to worse. As the exchange rates rose, so did the membership of the new Nazi Party of which, by 1923, had increased in excess of 55,000. The rise of the exchange rate was astonishing and crippling to Germany, as shown below.

Year	No of Marks to the US Dollar
1919	4
1921	75
1922	400
January 1923	18,000
July 1923	160,000
August 1923	1,000,000
November 1923	4,000,00,000

Life in Germany was becoming more and more difficult. Money was more or less worthless. Germans lost their life savings. Groceries cost billions of Marks and in many urban areas hunger riots broke out. When the Government decided to resume payment of the reparation debt in September 1923, bitter resentment and unrest swelled even more. Many Germans lost faith in the Government and turned to extremist organisations such as Nazism and Communism.

From the growing number of members within the Nazi Party, in 1921 Hitler created a private and unofficial army, a paramilitary organisation, named *Sturm Abteilung* (SA) meaning Storm Troopers but nicknamed 'Brownshirts'. The SA were mostly ex-soldiers and the unemployed. Hitler began turning them from a violent and unruly army to one which was organised and defined and of good reputation.

Germany was divided into individual states, each being run independently by a *Gauleiter* (District Governor). The Nazi Party was based in Munich in the state of Bavaria. Nazi Party members and Storm Troopers expected their leader to do something extreme to ensure changes to the country were made. By September 1923 Hitler had 3,000 troops trained and ready. He planned to kidnap the heads of the Bavarian Government and force them to accept him as their leader with a view to unifying the separately run states. He found out that on 8th November 1923 these men would be gathering with a group of businessmen at a Munich beer hall. A plan was set in place and The Storm Troopers burst into the beer hall. Hitler fired a single pistol shot at the ceiling shouting "Silence!" and two Government heads were abducted and taken away. It seemed the rebellion was going to plan and its perceived success culminated the next day in a triumphant march into Munich to take power. However, Police and Army reinforcements had been called in. A fight ensued and 16 Storm Troopers were killed. Hitler fled the scene but two days later was found, arrested and tried for high treason. He was sentenced to 5 years in prison.

It is well documented that Hitler devoted most of his time in prison to writing his memoir, in effect an autobiographical manifesto, which was published two years later. *Mein Kampf* (My Struggle) became the Nazi bible. Due to the fact that many were sympathetic to his cause, he was released after 8 months. On his release from prison, he realised that revolution was not the route to power so set about reorganising his Party with a view to proving the Nazi Party to be a viable option at the next election.

In 1925 Hitler established the *Schutzstaffel* (Protection Squadron), known as the SS. The squadron comprised the best of the SA and others. They were chosen for their 'racial purity', blind obedience and fanatical loyalty to Hitler with their black uniforms contrasting the 'brownshirts' of the SA. Heinrich Himmler was placed in charge of the 300 strong SS and by 1933 he had grown it to 35,000 active members. Along with the SA they became symbols of terror as they sought out and dealt with dissidents.

Whatever Adolf Hitler was doing, the Party was winning public acceptance as by 1925 membership had increased to 27,000. The Party continued to grow and, despite the next few years being known as the 'lean years', Party membership reached 130,000 in 1929 with 400,000 members of the SA.

The new German President, Paul von Hindenberg, was not sympathetic to the Nazi movement but Hitler continued to fine tune any problems with the principles of the Party and iron out discrepancies amongst the members with the aim of becoming a more and more exceptional Party for the way forward.

One of the reasons for their lack of success was that Germany seemed to be experiencing an upturn in the economy due to the introduction of a new currency. This recovery affected the population in a positive way and, with Nazi propaganda continuing to play on people's fears, the majority of the population began opting for a more moderate party.

However, the upturn was swiftly reversed due to the Wall Street Crash on the US stock exchange in October 1929 when American Banks needed immediate repayment of all loans, causing Germany's debts to grow exponentially due to increased lending. German industry lost all its finance and failed. More and more became unemployed. The 1million unemployed in 1928, by 1931 had risen to 3 million, only to double to 6 million by 1932. The Nazi Party realised they were able to use the country's bad fortune to their benefit.

Chapter 3

Family

Despite the huge numbers of unemployed and the terrible state of Germany's economy, Hildegard and her family did not suffer. Money was far from plentiful but they did not consider themselves poor or needy as they had enough to eat and they were able to continue to live in the simple manner to which they had always been accustomed. The family was part of a large network of relatives which included two sets of grandparents and numerous aunts, uncles and cousins, with the majority living in their own or nearby villages. The friendly village community, far away from major towns and cities, ensured that neighbours looked out for each other and were ready to share what they had to help those in need. Thankfully Josef had a reliable job which provided a reasonable wage and, due to growing their own fruits and vegetables, and with produce from their few animals, the family remained well fed and most of their needs were met.

Hildegard began her education at the local school aged six and a half and immediately embraced the experience. After all, she knew all the children, their families and their grandparents in their own and neighbouring villages. She fondly remembers the first day in her new school. "What a smart girl" said her mother as she stood back to inspect Hildegard after neatly braiding her hair. There was no school uniform but each girl was required to wear a *durndl* (gathered skirted) apron over their clothes, and Maria had made a crisp new apron in preparation for Hildegard's special day. On went her coat and boots and she set off excitedly on this fresh April morning striding out confidently ahead of her mother and Gretel. Lots of other children were walking in the same direction and smiles and waves and greetings were shared along the way.

Her mother led Hildegard into her classroom where the teacher was waiting at the front of a large room filled with several lines of school desks and chairs. As each child was shown to one of the little desks, the mothers were quickly ushered out. The class included children spanning ages 6 to 8, this being the start of their third school year for some. The teacher, from the front of the classroom, greeted the new children warmly and introduced herself and the rest of the class. She was smiling and spoke kindly. The children were asked to bow their heads and the teacher said a prayer to start the day. After taking their seats each new child was invited to the teacher's desk, one at a time, to receive a *wundertute* (wonder bag). This was a brightly coloured stiff paper cone, tied at the top with a bow and with a label showing the child's name. Hildegard remembered the teacher calling her name "Hildegard Scheitza", after which she walked to the front of the classroom to collect her gift. After taking it back to her desk and carefully untying the bow, she peered inside to find gifts such as pencils, chocolate, a ball, an orange, and other surprises. The children had no idea that their parents had each created and filled a cone for their own child and given it to the teacher the day before the start of term. This happy tradition made the first day of school extra special and the children would keep their *wundertute* as a memento.

On Sundays after church, the Scheitza family would visit the grandparents. Mostly they'd visit Maria's parents who lived in Dammern, a few kilometres away. They would travel the short distance on bicycles. Josef had a smart new bicycle with a seat on his crossbar for Hildegard whilst Maria had a seat on the back of hers for Gretel. Their mother always felt uncomfortable when visiting Josef's parents so visits were as rare as possible even though they basically lived next door.

Hildegard well remembers one of these rare visits, on the occasion of her paternal grandparents' golden wedding anniversary. It was a huge gathering which included the couple's 9 children, spouses and around 20 grandchildren. Hildegard and Gretel had recently been unwell with measles but they were now feeling much better and looking forward to a fun time with their cousins. However, even though Maria assured her mother-in-law that her granddaughters were fully recovered and, after a week, not contagious, *Grossmutter* (Grandmother) decided the girls felt feverish and could still have high temperatures so she sent them both to bed, causing them to miss the party downstairs. However, they soon cheered up the next morning when they heard that Grossmutter had given all the cousins some money to take home with them, and Hildegard and Gretel had not been forgotten. From then on, the sisters called her *'Reich Grossmutter'* (Rich Grandmother)!

When the girls were old enough to walk together, unattended by a parent, Hildegard and Gretel were occasionally required to visit two of their father's sisters who were maiden aunts. Tante Julie and Tante Annastasia (known as Tante Anna) were extremely fervent Catholics and they proudly and importantly rang the bells in the tiny village chapel each Sunday morning and on every 'holy day of obligation'. Although Tante Anna was quite friendly towards her nieces, Tante Julie was definitely not so. She was very critical and complained constantly. She would ask curtly "Have you been to church?" or "Is your mother not coming?"

The aunts adhered to a strict dress code which did not include hems above the knee or short sleeves. Tante Julie would say "Oh your mother has made new dresses for you I see. Why does she make them so short? Did she not have enough material? We should not see your elbow and we should not see your knee!" This conversation occurred on each visit, even though both girls had pulled their skirts down to below their knees and ensured their elbows were well hidden. Hildegard, in an effort to limit criticism, would remind Gretel to "Pull your skirt down. We are almost there!" on the walk to their house.

During the visit the sisters would dutifully and politely sit with the aunts and try to enjoy the buttermilk and bread they were given. Their mother did not like Tante Julie at all but was compelled to send her daughters to please her husband.

Thankfully most of her father's siblings were far from objectionable. One of his brothers and a sister had settled separately in Berlin with their families. Oncle Johann, or Oncle Hans as he was more usually called, was the favourite uncle. When Hildegard was 7 years old her father was given two free railway tickets to Berlin so he decided to take his elder daughter on a very special excursion. It was Christmas time and her mother had managed to buy Hildegard a smart red coat for the trip. Father and daughter stayed at the home of Oncle Hans, his wife Tante Anna and their three sons, and whilst in Berlin they also visited Tante Sopfie and her husband and their two children.

Josef took Hildegard on a day trip into Berlin's city centre. The huge buildings and the many shops selling beautiful items were unlike anything she had ever before seen. Brightly coloured Christmas lights lit up every street. It was a wonderful sight. There was no obvious sign of lack or poverty, at least not to a child on her first visit to a big city. One of the highlights was a visit to the department store where Oncle Hans worked, maintaining and keeping the lifts in good repair. The store assistants were dressed as Christmas elves and Hildegard had never seen so many toys on display. Decorations were draped across ceilings and walls with twinkling lights and sparkle everywhere she looked. She decided that Berlin must be the most magical place in the world. She'd had such a happy and glorious time that she hoped one day she'd have the opportunity to return. For Hildegard this had been a trip of a lifetime and one she would never forget.

The trip to Berlin had been a rare experience as, back home in Jaginne, Hildegard and Gretel seldom left their village. The exceptions were the infrequent visits to relatives who lived locally and the very occasional special treats when their mother needed to take her daughters into Carlsruhe to buy fabric, clothing or shoes. The sisters loved visits to Carlsruhe with its many different small shops and they were always pleased and enthusiastic to make the journey. One of these trips was especially planned as Mama had promised to buy a very excited Hildegard a red cardigan with gold buttons. She was so happy. But not so Gretel who also wanted a red cardigan with gold buttons but the answer from their mother had to be a very firm "No Gretel! You will have it for yourself soon enough!" The cardigan would eventually belong to Gretel when Hildegard grew too big for it and it would be passed down to the younger sister. That's how it worked. There was never enough money to be spent purely to keep a child happy. If Gretel needed a new cardigan, it would be bought from a cheaper shop as it didn't need to last that long due to there being no sibling to pass it on to! That's how it had to be, but so often Gretel was not happy with that rule!

Chapter 4

Village Life

The school year began in the spring, after Easter. During the spring and summer terms the school day would start at 7am and finish at 1pm giving Hildegard and Gretel long afternoons to enjoy. On most days they would go straight home for lunch. "We're home Mama!" the girls would call as they waved goodbye to their friends at the gate. Hildegard would be careful where she walked inside the gate as there could often be a stray hen which had somehow escaped from the chicken run. "Come on you. Back you go" she'd say as she picked up the complaining bird and popped her back into the coop. She would take that opportunity to check for eggs and more often than not she would find a few large fresh eggs the family could share for their lunch. The hens spent much of their time trying to escape and whenever successful they'd head straight for the house to pay a visit. They were very unruly chickens but great fun.

After the harsh winters of Eastern Europe, spring was always welcomed. The marguerites in the meadow would be in bud with expectations of another beautiful display in the summer, and as the trees came into leaf and wild flowers opened their buds in the hedgerows, winter would soon be forgotten. As summer approached, and the weather became warmer, Hildegard and her sister were able to spend lots of time playing and amusing themselves out of doors. The warm summer months at school were especially delightful as the children enjoyed nature lessons outside. Hildegard looked forward to nature lessons which included field trips to the nearby forest and lakes. The day before a field trip the teacher would ask all the children to bring a picnic lunch from home and mothers would pack bread and a slice of meat into greaseproof paper packages along with fruit and a drink to be carried in their rucksacks.

The children learned about the flowers and berries and fungi that grew in and around the forest - including which berries and mushrooms were edible and which were poisonous and shouldn't be touched. This was an important education as foraging was a source of food for Hildegard and the people of Jaginne. The school children learned the names of wild flowers and plants and on returning to the classroom they carefully drew and coloured pictures of the flora and fungi they had studied and wrote as much as they could remember about them.

At the end of each school day during the summer term, the children had plenty of time to fill. With their father working long hours at Carlsruhe Station, their mother was always grateful for help in the house or garden. Although priority was always given to homework or the learning of spellings straight after lunch, before having plenty of time to themselves to play or relax, she would generally have a chore or two for her daughters to complete. She would ask, "Hilde could you please feed the chickens and geese, and please take Gretel with you"; a task both girls always enjoyed.

Once a week was laundry day. The weekly wash would be soaked overnight and scrubbed the next morning on a washboard. The white items would be boiled in a very large pan on the stove with a blue rinse and then starched before being hung on the washing line. Seeing her clean and sparkling white sheets, bedding and tablecloths billowing in the breeze was a very satisfying sight for Maria after the lengthy process required to actually get them from laundry basket to washing line.

Hildegard's parents made very good use of their two acres of land and they were grateful they were able to grow food for their family. They were fortunate to be well fed and in good health. Unlike many poverty-stricken urban areas, life in Jaginne for Hildegard and her sister was pleasant and mostly untouched by what was going on in the country as a whole. On the occasions they visited Carlsruhe they began to notice propaganda posters pasted onto walls and fences, promising prosperity and a better life. They were everywhere you looked in the larger towns and were almost all printed on behalf of the Nazi Party. It all looked very exciting but Hildegard and her family took little heed of them as life for them was not so bad.

The land around the family's bungalow incorporated a garden and plenty of space for growing vegetables. There was a large field for potatoes and a field for growing wheat. In addition to poultry, two goats were kept for their milk, a pig, rabbits, a duck called Putse, some geese and a cat. One day each year the butcher would come and slaughter the pig. The girls were used to this as it happened every year. Papa would buy a pig and rear it for bacon. The butcher would cut the flesh into rashers and pork chops and joints. Some meat would be smoked for winter rations and some would be hung in the cellar to dry. Hildegard always ensured she didn't get attached to the pig and wouldn't name it. Pigs and poultry and rabbits were food, and that was that.

Twice a week her mother would cycle the 4km into Carlsruhe to buy groceries. Hildegard especially loved shopping day because Mama would bring home fresh bread. Whilst her grandmother like many baked her own, her mother preferred to buy their bread from the baker and bake her own cakes and buns instead. As well as the grocer she would visit the butcher, the greengrocer, the baker and the fishmonger for essential items. Vinegar and soused herrings would always be important items on the shopping list.

Hildegard and Gretel would sometimes be given a few coins as pocket money for carrying out various tasks for their mother. As well as feeding the animals Hildegard would clean inside the house whilst Gretel swept and tidied outside. The girls would carefully save their earnings for the occasions Mama would allow them to visit the village shop to spend it. Gretel would buy sweets and Hildegard would buy soused herrings!

For the village children the forest was also their summer playground. On sunny afternoons after school and at weekends Hildegard and her sister, along with other neighbourhood children, would head to the forest to play and gather berries. Hildegard was responsible for her younger sister and so often she would have to chase after her as Gretel had a mind of her own and could run fast for her age. Her strong-willed sister would head for the woods but she didn't know which fruits were to be picked and which were not. Hildegard took her responsibility seriously and ensured she kept her eyes on Gretel at all times. Gretel loved the game of running away knowing that her elder sister would catch her. Hildegard would then berate her, "Gretel, come on now. You know you should wait for me. I need to tell you what to pick." They picked edible mushrooms and fruit, which included wild strawberries, blueberries and blackberries in season. Hildegard felt very grown up, not only knowing which fruits and fungi were edible and which were poisonous but also knowing that she was helping with the family budget as much of what they picked would be sold.

The forest was large and the further it was ventured into many deer and rabbits could be seen, as well as wild boar. In July and August when all the berry varieties were ripe there were plenty of fruits to be foraged by adults and children alike. Having collected all they could carry, the pickers would head to the outer edge of the forest where a dealer would be stationed. The dealer would weigh each basket and pay the pickers accordingly. The produce would be taken to Berlin and Breslau (now Wroclaw) for selling on in the markets. Hildegard and Gretel picked as much as they could to please their mother who saved the money to buy new school clothes and boots for the coming winter months.

During summer holidays and weekends Hildegard and Gretel would often stay for several hours, first foraging and then playing in the forest with their friends. They would climb trees and scale the ladder into the tree house where they could see for miles around. The 'tree house' was actually a look out post for the forest ranger. There was also a cottage in the forest for the ranger to live in. He was permitted to shoot rabbits and deer and any other animal he came across. When visiting the forest for nature lessons with their teacher, the children weren't allowed to climb the ladder but after school and weekends it was a different matter. Also in the forest was a derelict wooden cabin which in days long ago included a fire in the middle of the floor situated directly under a chimney in the roof. It was once the home of previous forest rangers. On the walls were etched many names of local people dating back through generations. The children could point out their parents' and grandparents' and even great grandparents' names, as well as those of aunties and uncles and cousins.

As autumn arrived the fruit trees and bushes would be stripped bare of fruit, the leaves would fall and the weather begin to cool. The sisters' trips into the forest would now be used to gather extra wood for the stove which, as well as being employed for cooking and heating water, would be needed to provide warmth for the family during the coming winter. Josef would lead these excursions and the family would cut and collect as much wood as they could. They'd pile their hand wagon as high as possible with logs, dragging them home to be stored in the woodshed in preparation for the winter months. Winters in Eastern Germany were extreme, usually reaching sub-zero temperatures with heavy snowfall and extending to several months. Winters had to be prepared for.

Autumn was an especially busy time when Hildegard and Gretel would help their parents with the harvest. They were grateful for the help of neighbours, and they in turn would also help them and their grandparents with their harvesting. Hildegard wasn't so keen on this kind of heavy work as it caused pain in her back but she worked as hard as she could. There was plenty to do to help. There were tons of potatoes to be picked as well as hay to be cut. Her father would rake the hay together in large heaps and then turn it over every other day until dry. As well as being hard physical work it was also a sociable time with neighbours chatting and laughing together as they worked.

The geese reared by the family were kept for their meat, fat and feathers. Autumn was the time of year for many to be culled. The goose meat and fat were carefully preserved and stored and her father would then pluck the feathers, remove the hard central ribs and collect the soft down in bags. The feathers would be used to make *federbetts* (feather beds or duvets) and pillows. As well as ensuring their homes were always equipped with adequate bedding, it was a tradition for parents to make a feather bed and pillows for sons and daughters as wedding presents.

Hildegard's parents would prepare for winter throughout the summer and autumn months to ensure the family were well prepared to efficiently adjust to the change of season. Winter would stretch from early December until the end of March. Each cold winter morning Maria would call "Hilde! Gretel! Breakfast is ready!" Josef would have left for work much earlier and the two girls and their mother would sit at the kitchen table together to eat a warm and hearty meal of porridge made with goat's milk. It was always goats' milk. Never cows'. Goats' milk was considered so much better for you. Mother would have coffee with her porridge and then it was time to get ready for school. Layers of warm clothes were necessary, including hand knitted woollen stockings, knitted and fur edged hats and gloves and thick woollen coats. Life in East Germany comprised warm, sunny summers and harsh winters.

Maria and Josef ensured that by December, when the snow began to fall and temperatures were freezing, their family had a cool room full of provisions to get them through the cold winter. Enough dried and smoked meats, potatoes in abundance, and plenty of flour from the mill which they'd exchanged for the grain harvested from their wheat field. Jar upon jar of fruit preserves filled the shelves, all made from their home-grown apples, pears and cherries and the strawberries, blueberries and blackberries Hildegard and Gretel had picked in the forest. And, of course, there were also many large jars of traditional freshly pickled sauerkraut, prepared from the cabbages they had grown and harvested.

By January and February there would be at least 600mm of snow on the ground. Each morning, warmed by their breakfast porridge, Hildegard and her sister would put their books into their school bags and set off on the 2kms to school, their thick fur boots sinking into the freshly fallen snow. School started at 8am during the winter. The girls would then make their way home again at 2pm for lunch and to spend the rest of the afternoon amusing themselves in the house. On occasional days they would stay at school longer for extra needlework lessons when they would take a sandwich for lunch. But most days they would arrive home to a wonderful and very welcome bowl of steaming hot vegetable soup, perhaps with a chunk of bacon. Or pea soup made with dried peas. Later, when Papa returned home from work, meat would always be included as part of their evening meal.

Wonderful tasty meat. They would eat roast chicken, pork or beef. There would often be freshly cooked potato pancakes which consisted of grated potatoes mixed with flour and eggs and fried in a skillet. And *klosel*, which was a dish of raw potato plunged into boiling water and mashed. And there were usually plenty of green vegetables, including cabbage and brussels sprouts, from the garden. And pancakes. They had them often as there were always plenty of eggs and flour. Blancmange was also a regular and much enjoyed dessert and their mother would bake apple and cherry cakes. Unlike many fellow countrymen and women in the towns and cities, the Scheitza family were never hungry.

Throughout the winter months there was little playing outside as it was far too cold so the girls would amuse themselves inside and use their imaginations to dream up various games. Dressing up was always a favourite and sometimes the sisters would make up a play and perform it in the evenings for their parents. Their father had built the girls a beautiful dolls house which they would play with for hours. Should they get bored there was always homework to be done and spellings to be learned.

Chapter 5

The German Government

Germany had been a Constitutional Federal Republic (The Weimar Republic) since 1918 but by the early 1930s the current Coalition Government was failing on every level. Due to the terrible state of the economy and loss of industry in Germany following the Great War, there was much infighting amongst the heads of the parties involved and there were many resignations. At this time the Nazi Party had grown to the extent of not only becoming the largest party, but being recognised as possible saviours by the population at this time of great hardship.

In January 1933, Germany's President, Paul von Hindenburg, appointed the role of Chancellor to Adolf Hitler, head of the growing and popular Nazi Party who promised to bring an end to the economic problems and the poverty and suffering of much of the German population. However, the main reason for Hitler's appointment was that President von Hindenburg and the previous Chancellor von Papen were of the view that Hitler was weak and they would be able to control him to do things their way.

Hitler, though, was no one's puppet. He had plans of his own, the ultimate aim of which was to bring the country to a place of complete independence from other countries as well as being solvent, strong, an economic success and a force to be reckoned with. To do this he needed, first of all, to cut the unemployment figures drastically. Now he was Chancellor he immediately set to work building factories, roads (the autobahn), hospitals and schools to provide more jobs. He also encouraged a vibrant car manufacturing industry. And the economy started to grow.

Part Two

1933 – 1938

Chapter 6

Chancellor Hitler and His 25-Point Plan

President von Hindenburg soon realised that Adolf Hitler was not going to be as easy to control as he had hoped. As Chancellor, Hitler was determined to start putting his well thought out '25-Point Plan' into action. He began by taking steps to improve the country's industry, thus providing employment for all as he held the belief that every citizen should earn a livelihood and live well, provided they stayed within the limits of the Party rules. Much of the plan seemed good and helpful to the population but some aspects sparked confusion and concern. Some of the more questionable ideas were; 1) Citizenship was a big part of the Plan. Any person living in Germany but not of German blood (Aryan) would be considered an alien, and 2) The economy would come under the control of the Government, with the law and media also being subject to the strict Nazi regime. Most were left wondering what constituted a pure Aryan German and would the German people be expected to hand over most, if not all, of their freedoms. But, at such a time of extreme lack, teamed with intense indoctrination via propaganda, it was hoped that the new Chancellor's plans might well prove to be to the country's benefit.

Hitler, determined to realise his great plans for Germany, intended to eliminate all threats and hindrances that might prove problematic. One of the first steps towards this was the banning of all other political parties and to oppress all political and racial enemies of the Nazi party. He had already established the SA and the SS but this wasn't enough to rid the country of dissenters so he commissioned Hermann Goering to create a secret police force. *The Gestapo* (Secret State Police) became infamous for the use of intimidation, coercion and torture. As well as tapping telephones and opening mail to seek out antagonists they would also, dressed in civilian clothes, mingle unnoticed among groups of people whilst listening to conversations. Anyone who was perceived to be an enemy of the State would be eliminated without trial.

Hitler's plans to create a population of pure Aryan Germans had already caused an exodus of many Jews out of the country to Mandatory Palestine, the Jewish national home, which had been created as promised in the Balfour Declaration of 1917.

Although antisemitic ideas had been adopted by some for many years, in April 1933 Hitler began the systematic persecution of all Jewish people. The perpetration of his Nazi belief, that only pure ethnic Germans should be citizens and that all Jews should be financially ruined, began with the command for the complete boycott of all Jewish shops and businesses, with many of their properties hitherto vandalised. Authorities began stripping Jews of all property, freedoms and rights under the new law, whilst all Jewish people were ousted from public office and professions and all Jewish civil servants, lawyers and teachers were sacked.

As well as preventing the Jewish population from earning an honest living, Hitler also ruled that Jewish children could only be taught in Jewish schools. Meanwhile all German mainstream schoolchildren were told to believe that Jews were *Untermensch* (subhuman).

In May 1933 Hitler ordered that all books not in full agreement with the Nazi point of view would be banned or burned. These actions resulted in the exodus of more and more Jews from Germany.

Propaganda was a very successful tool to ensure the population were totally behind the Nazi regime and Hitler's plans for the country and its people. Joseph Goebbels had been given the responsibility of creating and distributing Hitler's propaganda 10 years before in 1923 and he continued to carry out the task with great enthusiasm. His posters were to be seen in towns everywhere. Nazi propaganda promoting Hitler's government, with slogans such as 'Germany Awakens!' 'The NAZI Party!' and 'Work, Freedom and Bread!' were all designed to influence public opinion.

It was Goebbels who had the idea to stage a Nazi Rally comprising a gathering of the growing Military, members of the Party and youth groups brought together to demonstrate to German countrymen the strength, order and power of the Nazi Party. The first rally had taken place in 1923 and was not especially impactful. Not discouraged though, as the Nazi Party grew, Goebbels continued to promote his idea and by the time Adolf Hitler came to power the rally was gaining interest and was becoming the spectacular event he had hoped for, exhibiting the discipline and order of the new Military as they marched in sync in their immaculate uniforms. The rally became bigger and better each year, eventually being carried out at the enormous purpose-built grounds in Nurembourg, with rousing speeches given by Hitler and other Nazi members. As well as an encouragement to the German population it was a way of showing the world that Germany was now a force to be reckoned with.

To achieve his aims Hitler planned to create a totalitarian state with himself as the dictator bearing absolute power over every German and over every business and organisation, even the law and religious practices.

All trade unions were banned and all workers had to join the Nazi led German Labour Front which promised to look after them, as long as they complied. But there were those who knew the whole story behind this façade of wealth and opportunity and were unhappy with the excessive control over everything including the press and public opinion.

Many welcomed the changes as money was becoming more plentiful, employment was increasing and the country seemed to be improving in every way.

Hitler had his ear to the ground at all times and he was determined that nothing would thwart his plans of a Nazi dictatorship for Germany with him at the helm. However, he became aware that some members of the SA (*Sturmabteilung* – German 'Assault Division') were becoming somewhat of a threat to his planned regime. His old comrade and leader of the SA, Ernst Rohm and others were creating tension as they held views other than his and there was talk of a coup being planned. Fearful of losing control, in July 1934, he ordered all SA members to attend an evening meeting in a hotel in Bavaria. He immediately placed Rohm and other SA leaders under arrest. Rohm was given the choice of suicide or murder. Refusing the suicide offer he was shot by SS guards. 85 men in total were arrested and all shot. In addition, it is said that around 400 men were killed at various locations; men who proved a threat, on what Hitler later named The Night of the Long Knives (after a popular song of the time!).

Soon after, Hitler made a speech stating "In this hour I was responsible for the fate of the German people, and therefore I became the supreme judge of the German people. I gave the order to shoot the ringleaders in this treason." Hitler had wiped out all opposition within his own party, leaving the way clear for him to rule and lead as he had planned with no interference from troublemakers.

Chapter 7

Changes

Meanwhile in Jaginne, most villagers were not particularly interested in Nazi propaganda, and generally not concerned by it as they were busy with their farms and jobs and families, and their lives continued to be mostly unaffected by the new regime. On occasions, when venturing further afield, they might see the political slogans and were hopeful that the leaders of their government would carry out the promises made to give the population a much-improved future.

The first time Hildegard became personally aware that changes and influences to their everyday lives were being made was one Monday morning as she and her friends filed into their Roman Catholic school. She immediately noticed that some very explicit alterations had been made within the school building. The walls, usually covered with religious iconic pictures, were now adorned with portraits of Hitler, Goering and Goebbels. No religious pictures or statues were to be seen. Then, as the students gathered in their classrooms at the start of the day, their usual morning greeting to their teacher of *"Gruss Gott"* ("Good Day") was suddenly to be changed to *"Heil Hitler"* ("Hail Hitler"), along with what eventually became a practiced-till-perfect Nazi salute. The salute became essential when naturally greeting friends and neighbours and entering shops. Even the postman knocking on doors would greet each person with the salute whilst proclaiming *"Heil Hitler"*. Although not mandatory, those seen not honouring their leader in this specific way were often suspected to be dissidents and arrested so it became a habit of the entire population, for their personal safety's sake.

Another change was the name of their village. Right out of the blue Jaginne was renamed Damweide! Other than these random changes, the lives of Hildegard, her family and their village were not unduly affected. Due to the positive-sounding propaganda most thought Hitler to be a wonderful man whose aim was to bring wealth and prosperity to Germany and the future looked bright, so the Nazi salute was the least they could do to honour this great man and his promises.

In his days as leader of the early Nazi Party Hitler created *Hitler-Jungend, Bund Deutscher Arbeiterjugend (*Hitler Youth, League of German Worker Youth). Known as HJ, this was in effect a paramilitary organisation for boys in Germany with the motto 'Blood and Honour'. Its aim was to ensure the future of Nazi Germany through the young by indoctrinating children and teenagers in Nazi ideology and racism. A threat to this new initiative was Baden-Powell's very popular international Boy Scouts Movement, so Hitler banned the Scouts! *Hitler-Jungend* would include the sports and camping and hiking element of the original Boy Scouts' activities, with the addition of weapons training, assault course circuits and military tactics.

For the girls there was the *Bund Deutscher Madel* (The League of German Maidens) which was compulsory for every girl to join and wear the uniform of white blouse and black skirt. Hildegard was very happy to belong to The League and dressed in the compulsory uniform but she was disappointed to have no group to meet with in the village. However, there were lessons in school which followed the teaching of the League, which included domesticity ensuring that each girl was fully equipped to become a good wife and mother.

The idealistic Adolf Hitler, to create and increase a population of pure Germans, introduced inducements encouraging all ethnic German women to have as many children as possible. Each mother giving birth to a child would be given a monetary reward. The more children one had the more the financial reward.

Recognising the changes but unhindered by what was going on in the political arena, life went on and Hildegard continued to enjoy school. As well as nature lessons she particularly enjoyed needlework, arithmetic and religion. She did not like history and geography. Literature was a favourite and she very much liked to learn poetry by heart. She was particularly fond of the writings of

Joseph Freiherr von Eichendorff, a popular poet and playwright who belonged to one of the Romantic movements of the day, and who was a native Silesian.

On 2nd August 1934 it was announced that, at the age of 87 President Hindenburg had died. It was immediately declared that Adolf Hitler would become the next leader of the country, combining the Chancellorship with the Presidency. Every member of the Military was required to take an oath of allegiance. A vote was taken by the people and the strength of Nazi propaganda ensured that on 19th August Hitler was formally elected and, deciding to do away with both titles of Chancellor and President, he chose to call himself *Fuhrer* (Leader), defining his role as the absolute authority in Germany's Third Reich.

Later that year, in the winter of 1934 when Hildegard was 10 years old, the bottom fell out of her world. Her dear loving Papa had a life changing accident on the railway where he worked. Josef held an administrative post in the railway station office, but on this particular day he was unusually asked to help out with coupling the wagons. Somehow, suddenly, he had a terrible fall and suffered an extremely bad injury to his head. He was rushed to hospital where eventually, and to his family's great relief, they were told his life was not in danger. However, he would need to stay in hospital for further investigation as there were problems indicating possible brain damage. After several long weeks of tests showing no improvement, the family were informed that at this point nothing more could be done to enable Josef to live a normal life. He had no memory and had lost his power of speech. For now, Josef needed to remain in hospital. Hildegard, her mother and sister were heartbroken. The hospital was a distance away and the family took the train to visit as much as they could. They would sit by his bedside and hold his hand. The sisters would say "Hello Papa" but he didn't recognise them on those early visits and he couldn't speak or respond so they just cried, their mother cried, and their dear father cried too.

There was no way of knowing how extensive the damage to Josef's brain actually was and how long it would be until, if ever, he would be well enough to return to his family. In actuality it would be many months before Josef regained his memory and the ability to speak again but it would be many years before he'd be well enough to return home as he was not in full control of his decisions and would therefore be a danger to himself.

As time progressed it was decided that Josef should be transferred to a convalescent home. The home, run by nuns, was comfortable and homely. He was very well looked after and was as happy as he could be in the circumstances. Unfortunately, the family had no choice but to reduce their number of visits as the home was much further afield and the increased cost of train fares more difficult to find, but they made the journey as often as they could. Subsequent visits showed gradual improvements as Josef began to recognise his wife and then his daughters and communication became a little easier. In time he was given occupational tasks to help his brain and his movement. It was a very sad time for them all, not knowing if and when Josef would ever be well enough to return home and live a normal life. His family missed him terribly.

Life had taken a sudden and difficult turn for the Scheitza family with the additional problem of the loss of Josef's regular income. He had worked for the railway for 20 years and had paid into a pension, but they only received half as Maria wasn't a widow. Germany was already suffering due to the drop in worth of the Mark and coupons were being carefully designated to people according to their needs. Maria was compelled to tell the authorities that they produced their own meat and also some milk and butter from their goat after which coupons were duly deducted. Thankfully they were still able to sell the fruits they picked in the forest which helped a little. Sometimes they would have to stay the whole day in the forest foraging. Maria took a small rent from neighbours for the use of their stable and she worked for neighbouring farmers to increase their income. When she realised her excellent sewing skills could be put to good use, she took sewing and dressmaking orders to help further. She also worked in the forest preparing ground to plant new trees. If she ever heard of the need for a paid worker, Maria applied for the job.

One of Maria's brothers owned a farm in nearby Dammern and he would sometimes pay a visit and bring food provisions. The maiden aunts would occasionally come to help out and Hildegard's grandparents would be ready to provide food as and when needed whilst ensuring the family always had a good supply of bread and milk and butter. Maria was busy from dawn to dusk with the running of the home and tending animals and crops as well as dressmaking for neighbours and other means of earning money. Thankfully the family had wood for the stove for cooking and heating; lighting was provided by petroleum lamps in the house and lanterns for outside and in the sheds and there were no taxes or rent to pay so there were not too many bills.

Maria, to whom it was of great importance that her family were well dressed, was determined to do all she could to buy fabric and shoes when needed for herself and her daughters. In her 'spare' time, she would continue to knit and sew for her family, and any help with this by her mother was gratefully received. Both were very skilled seamstresses.

In the autumn the hard work of harvest and preparing for winter was now down to her and, with her children doing their best to help, Maria would make the regular trips into the forest with their little wagon to collect all the wood they would need for the cold months ahead.

Hildegard would often ask her mother "When will Papa come home?" The stoic reply was always the same, "He's not well enough to come home." It was such a sad and difficult time for the family.

Chapter 8

The New Regime

Adolf Hitler's popularity was growing due to his many promises and the gradual improvement to the country's economy. Wherever you turned there were more and more posters on walls and in windows, and leaflets were posted into everyone's home displaying Nazi propaganda. The intense brainwashing was so convincing that most of the population were glad to continue to put their trust in the new leadership. However, there were a growing number of Germans who did not trust this new leader and despised all he stood for. They recognised Hitler as a power-crazy dictator, determined to ensure that the entire population of Germany was subject to him and his rules. Loyalty to the Fuhrer was essential and anyone who dared to oppose him would be harshly dealt with.

Hitler organised Himmler's SS to oversee the running of the *Gestapo* and the *Sicherheitsdienst* (the Intelligence Agency of the SS). The Gestapo had become very successful at seeking out any found to be opposed in any way to the Nazi regime. Retribution was harsh as anyone who could be accused of being an enemy of the State would be immediately imprisoned and tortured or shot. The lives of Germans were becoming subject to control by terror as the Gestapo effectively and insidiously lived and moved amongst the population countrywide, gathering information from ordinary people, many of whom were happy to inform on their fellow countrymen.

Nazis controlled everything: the law, the press, radio broadcasts, the propaganda ridden mass rallies and sports events. Everything. The 1936 Olympic Games were especially set up to demonstrate Nazi Germany's strength and power. They displayed new technology like television cameras and even the first stop clock to show their superiority to the world.

Even arts and culture were under Nazi control as they stripped galleries and museums of paintings they claimed were 'degenerate'. All books representing ideologies opposed to Nazism, and those written by socialists, pacifists and Jews, including those of Albert Einstein, were burnt. Certain plays and films and music were deemed subversive and banned from being publicly played or shown. All artistic license had to disappear except for those promoting the physical and military power and popularity of the German Aryan race.

Most Germans believed Hitler's hype despite the many freedoms and rights that were being slowly taken away from them. The effective propaganda caused the majority to unwittingly find themselves happy to live their lives in subservience to the Fuhrer. At least life was better in the sense that there were some economic improvements and more jobs due to the many new factories being created all over the country. There was much building work as Hitler encouraged new and elaborate constructions in the cities and major towns. Compared to the recession the majority were believing that now at least they had security for themselves and their families and their futures.

Hitler even took control of the Protestant Church. This was far from a popular move amongst Protestants and a pastor named Martin Niemoller led a group of pastors to form the Confessional Church in opposition to the newly named and controlled National Reich Church. He was of course, captured and taken to a concentration camp. 800 other protestant pastors and 400 catholic priests were labelled dissidents and were detained in camps until their eventual release when the war finally came to an end.

Schools were instructed to teach age-appropriate propaganda to convince young people of Hitler's greatness and to encourage them to grow up to be active Nazi Party members. Children were given books to read which taught antisemitism so, like little sponges, they believed from an early age that Jews were bad.

For some enquiring youth, however, it was a different story. Hitler Youth typically included some young people who were intelligent enough to question these new ideals and strict discipline. Various opposition groups had started to spring up, bringing together those of like mind. Many of these young men thought for themselves, bravely and determinedly rejecting Nazi values and purposefully doing all the things that were strictly banned, such as printing anti-Nazi leaflets, painting anti-Nazi slogans on walls, drinking alcohol, dancing to banned jazz music and singing German pre-Nazi folk songs. Though much of the rebellion escaped punishment, rarely did it go unnoticed by the Gestapo as groups were regularly raided and dispersed. However, a large uprising stemmed from two young students in Munich University who circulated anti-Nazi leaflets and, after leading a march through Munich, they were arrested and sentenced to the guillotine. Then in the Rhineland 700 were arrested at an anti-Nazi meeting and when one member of the youth resistance killed a Gestapo chief, 12 of the 700 were publicly hanged. Strong and extreme messages from Himmler's SS to German youth that any opposition would not be tolerated.

Most German resistance to the Nazi regime however was made up of many small, isolated and clandestine groups of people. It had to be this way so as not to draw attention to themselves. The intent of these small groups was to subtly bring down this evil regime by the secret planning and carrying out of random acts of sabotage for the purpose of standing up for freedom and to disencumber the strict running of their country. Later, from the start of WWII the disclosure of information about Nazi armaments factories to the allies would be an important task for the resistance. All anti-Nazi meetings and plots were held in secret including the covert printing of anti-Nazi leaflets and graffiti, plans to overthrow Hitler, and the slowing down of work to hinder the progress of the regime.

Every citizen and every organisation became subject to the Government and to not go along with their ideology was risky. Suddenly a freak accident would happen to someone, or a neighbour would be shot or sent to a concentration camp. Approximately 77,000 German citizens were killed for some form of resistance. Concentration camps were built to incarcerate those resisting Nazism, as well as all Socialists and Communists. Tens of thousands of Germans were arrested and taken to these camps for questioning, torture and hard labour due to being suspected of or engaged in opposition.

It was believed but never proven that Hildegard's father, Josef Scheitza, was involved in a small local anti-Nazi group which was loosely connected to his brother Hans in Berlin. Some thought that either his opinions or perhaps an act or plan of revolt had been uncovered and he had been made to pay by his terrible, sudden 'accident' at work. After all, why was he found in such a bad way between the rail carriages when his job was in the station office? Although they didn't understand it at the time, Hildegard and her family could eventually hold their heads up in pride knowing that Josef had held such high morals and principles to put his life in danger.

Although Josef's accident had completely altered the family's dynamic and made life much harder for them all, and though they missed his presence every single day, in time Maria came to realise that she was coping and doing very well, all things considered. She and her daughters were overjoyed when they finally heard the good news from the convalescent home that Josef's health and condition appeared to be stabilising. As well as being able to speak again there were signs of improvement to his mind and memory. As he became more able, the nuns at the home set him to work in one of the workshops they ran for patient rehabilitation. Locals would bring in items that needed mending such as sewing machines and broken furniture so that, as well as serving the community, the patients were receiving excellent occupational therapy.

Chapter 9

School in Nazi Germany

Other than her father's dreadful accident, there were very few obvious changes to Hildegard and Gretel's lives as they continued to help their mother and enjoy their school days. Hildegard had a very good memory, which served her well all her life. In the classroom she had no problem learning the scriptures off by heart and confidently reciting verses word for word. She loved to write plays which would be performed on the school stage. Her mother helped make the costumes and friends would set up the stage. Sometimes the plays included singing parts. The teachers so enjoyed one such play that they arranged for the higher school to watch it as well.

Whilst Protestant church leaders who refused to preach in line with Hitler's rules were being arrested and sent to concentration camps, their Catholic school was able to continue as normal as did their church services; this being due to the fact that Hitler was himself a Catholic. When Hildegard was 11 years old the local priest was celebrating his Golden Jubilee since taking Holy Orders. It was also Palm Sunday. At a special mass, being the eldest child in the Middle Class, Hildegard was chosen to stand by the altar rail holding a gold crown which sat on a velvet cushion. She was flanked on each side by several school friends who were all holding palm crosses. After mass there was a celebration in the church garden where she read aloud a poem, and later in the evening there was a party where the festivities continued.

Subtle and gradual changes were happening to what children were being taught in schools. It eventually became obvious that every school lesson had now in some way been altered to reflect Nazi ideology. Each schoolchild was to take part in five one-hour sessions of physical exercise and sports per week to train and form them into strong and healthy young athletes. As well as having their own sports day they also attended an annual Sportsfest where several schools would come together to compete against each other. Children from Hildegard's school would travel a few miles to Damratsch for Sportsfest as they had a larger playing field. There were various competitions and races and it was always an enjoyable and fun day.

History lessons included a course on the rise of the Nazi Party and Biology lessons taught children Nazi racial theories of evolution. Added to the curriculum was a new subject: Race Study and Ideology dealing with the Aryan ideal and antisemitism. All lessons were set to cunningly brainwash young minds.

Meanwhile the League of German Maidens were training girls in domesticity and preparing them for marriage, housewifery and motherhood, whilst every boy, under Nazi rule, had no choice but to join Hitler Youth when they reached 14 years of age. Hitler Youth was appealing to the young with its varied activities and an annual holiday which most boys would not have had the opportunity to experience, but its main aim was to indoctrinate boys into the politics of Nazism and to train them physically with a view to their joining the Military when they reached 18.

Hildegard and her peers were oblivious to the real nature of these changes and in their innocence could not see them as anything but good.

With the progression of each of the sisters into the Upper Class, Hildegard, and in time Gretel, were able to enjoy needlework lessons and both girls became proficient needlewomen. They first learnt embroidery stitching including cross stitch, backstitch and herringbone. Between them the sisters made lots of samplers and later handkerchiefs using very fine cotton crocheted edging with embroidery. They made cushion covers and table mats and mats for dressing tables with crochet frilled edging for Christmas presents. They also learned the very important skill of knitting and both sisters, along with their mother, as part of the preparations for the coming winter, would make woollen stockings, wool and fur hats and gloves, as well as cardigans, warm undergarments and socks. Most of everything the family wore was either hand knitted, sewn or crocheted.

All kinds of useful skills were taught in the school needlework lessons and when the students were proficient enough at stitching, they could progress to dressmaking. The first item they were required to make in the dressmaking class was an apron which would be used during their school cookery lessons. As they became more experienced, they made themselves dresses and even created their own dress patterns.

Hildegard especially remembered a dress she made for Gretel. It was a red and white checked durndl skirted dress with a square neckline which she trimmed with lace. She also added a lace trim around the hem. It was a traditional dress that fitted Gretel perfectly.

The village school taught around 100 children, their ages ranging from 6 to 15. The school was divided into three classes – Under Class for children aged 6 to 8, Middle Class for 9 to 11 year-olds and Upper Class for ages 12 to 14, each comprising a little over 30 children. Hildegard's teacher in the Upper Class was Mr Franz Novak who she liked very much. She was glad he was able to continue teaching in the school as, when the Nazis came to power, many teachers who wouldn't tow the party line were sacked. He lived in the School House with his wife and baby girl whose name was Gisela Maria Renate. Hildegard always liked those names and thought, if she ever had a little girl of her own, she would choose those names. She would often see baby Gisela in the village being pushed along by her mother in her cane pram.

After Josef's accident, Mr Novak had sympathy for the sisters as he knew they were having a difficult time managing without their father. He would sometimes make up little stories to make them smile. He'd say he'd passed their house on his bicycle and had seen a cat sitting in their window box amongst the geraniums. Simple and personal kindnesses that both girls appreciated.

Hildegard, being the eldest in the class would be asked by Mr Novak to oversee the classroom whilst he went to lunch or for a coffee break. She really enjoyed being in charge and was happy to have the responsibility.

Chapter 10

Hitler Determined to Achieve His Goals

Now that Adolf Hitler was in power, he was determined to concentrate on his goals: At the top of his list was to restore to Germany what once belonged to Germany by firstly incorporating all previously claimed lands in surrounding territories which were still largely populated by ethnic Germans. Also of extreme importance to him was his dream to create a new racial order in Europe dominated by the German "master race". He planned to reverse all the terms of the Treaty of Versailles. He had won the hearts of the German population by promising them these new ideals with promises to build a new, successful and expanded Germany populated only by pure Germans. His Military would be second to none. He would rule with a first class, well equipped and well-trained Army, Navy and Airforce behind him. Germany would excel under his rule.

The burdens put upon Germany by The Treaty of Versailles were a continued thorn in Hitler's flesh. Important German land had been lost due to reparations penalties. The Treaty had been debated, agreed and signed by 'The Big Three' victors of The Great War, namely Woodrow Wilson of the United States, David Lloyd George of Great Britain and George Clemencau of France. It marked the end of that very bloody war with a death toll of 20million with 21million casualties and it comprised 440 Articles determining demands on the German Government for reparations and punishment due to the carnage and excessive war damage done to, in particular France and Great Britain.

The Treaty had been signed in The Hall of Mirrors at the Palace of Versailles, France, and included two forced signatures by Germans, as none had been invited to attend. The Articles basically ripped Germany apart by the handing over or handing back of land to France and Poland in particular, the confiscation of all African colonies and giving them to the League of Nations from which they were hitherto expelled, with a reduction of the German Military to a mere 100,000 men. The Airforce was to be immediately dismantled and the Navy restricted to only six battleships, with no submarines.

The huge reparation payments amounting to £6.6 billion provided Germany with a debt of 269bn gold Marks, the equivalent of around 100,000 tonnes of gold. In January 1923, after struggling to keep up the payments for the debt, Germany defaulted and the French Army, in response, had moved into Germany's Ruhr area, taking full occupation which included the takeover of all high-quality farmlands and the coal and iron mining industries, to make up for the unpaid debts to them. The economy suffered and recession set in.

The German population had been hit hard for their sins during the Great War and the country as a whole felt the punishments to be extreme, unfair and harsh as they didn't agree that they had started the war.

Between 1933 and 1938 Hitler was seriously attempting to throw off all restrictions imposed by the Treaty of Versailles and reverse the rules. He was planning to incorporate territories with ethnic German populations into the Reich (the German Empire) and acquire a vast new empire in Eastern Europe whilst forming alliances. He was sure he could persuade other states to participate in the final solution.

He had begun by making pacts with neighbouring countries, such as a non-aggression pact with Poland, re-acquiring various territories, signing a Naval pact with Great Britain, creating a coalition with Italy and a pact with Japan. These countries were giving Hitler what he wanted to keep the peace. There was a general appeasement policy to prevent him from going to war, the thinking being that Germany's new leader should be allowed to believe that what he wanted was reasonable and when he was satisfied then he would stop.

Austria was also on Hitler's hit list and in February 1938 he pressurised the Austrian Chancellor into signing the German-Austrian Agreement which allowed Nazi members to become part of the Austrian Cabinet. Then in March he sent troops in to annexe Austria to Germany.

Hitler's next step was for the incorporation of the Sudetenland region of Czechoslovakia into the Reich, most of the population being ethnic Germans and many of whom claimed they were being treated like second class citizens since breaking with Germany after the Great War. Hitler's demands for Sudetenland caused huge friction with Edvard Benes, the Czechoslovakian Prime Minster, who was standing firm. In September 1938 the British Prime Minister Neville Chamberlain stepped in and met with Hitler in southern Germany to try and calm the situation between the two leaders. Hitler seemed to listen and agree. But a week later he changed his mind and decided to stick to his original plan. The Munich Conference was immediately called and at the end of the month Chamberlain, Italian Prime Minister Benito Moussolini, and Edouard Daladier the French Prime Minister, met with Adolf Hitler for a four-power peace summit to discuss the situation and try to come to an agreement. Though the conference did not include the leaders of the Soviet Union or Czechoslovakia itself, an agreement was agreed and signed enabling Hitler to claim Sudetenland – another act of appeasement to keep Europe from going to war. Benes resigned as Prime Minister and Neville Chamberlain returned to Britain to cheers as he waved the agreement for the world to see, believing this to be confirmation that war had been averted.

The Nazi belief that Germany must acquire and control more *Lebensraum* (living space) in the east, Hitler realised, would require war and as such he had begun to prepare for it as soon as he came to power. Remilitarisation had been defiantly going against every Military restriction of the Treaty of Versailles and, so far, 17,000 Jews had been expelled from the country. His plan to extend Germany's borders and create a perfect, independent and successful Ayran empire was well under way. With the Munich Conference now securing him Sudetenland, Adolf Hitler realised that Britain and France were weak.

Part Three

1939 - 1941

Chapter 11

World War II

In March 1939, despite the Munich Agreement giving him Sudetenland, Adolph Hitler invaded Czechoslovakia, hitherto dismembering the whole country and establishing German control of Czech lands.

All single men aged between 20 and 22 were conscripted to 6 months training.

Hitler continued gaining the trust of his geographic neighbours and in May 1939 he and Mussolini signed the "Pact of Steel", a formal Military Alliance between Germany and Italy.

In August 1939 Hitler and Stalin signed The Molotov-Ribbentrop Pact – declaring zero aggression between Germany and the Soviet Union with an additional secret agreement to divide Poland between the two nations.

Meanwhile, due to the Nazi regime, many ethnic Germans living in the west of Poland were losing their jobs and being treated very badly due to being suspected as Fifth Columnists. They were considered to be the enemy in Poland and all German language newspapers had been banned. Hitler, aware of the division and with no need to fear Soviet intervention, planned his next move.

On 1st September 1939 Hitler attacked Poland in order to, allegedly, "rescue the ethnic German population of that country from oppression". Two days later Poland's allies, Britain and France, declared war against Germany, this signalling the beginning of World War II.

Poland took immediate revenge on Germany by gathering every ethnic German, 15,000 in all, and marching them through the streets of Polish towns to be spat on, verbally abused and have rubbish and bricks thrown at them before being led into the internment camps of Central Poland. Many were shot as spies.

Such was the animosity that had grown between the two countries.

As soon as war was declared, Hildegard's Oncle Hans sent his son Norbert from their home in Berlin to stay with his brother Josef's family in Jaginne as Berlin was bound to be a prime target for enemy bombings. Norbert was Oncle Hans' youngest son. His two older sons were expecting to be called up into the army but, as Norbert was too young, Oncle Hans felt it safer for him to be as far away as possible from Berlin and his brother's home in Jaginne seemed the best and safest place for him. Maria was very happy with the arrangement. Norbert was not only a clever and well-educated young man but he was also a gifted musician. It was arranged for him to attend the High School in Carlsruhe so that he could continue with his education. Hildegard and Gretel were more than pleased their cousin had come to stay and he greatly lifted their spirits.

Hitler now called for all males aged 18 to 41 to immediately leave their homes to fight. Anyone found to be avoiding the call up would be found and shot!!

In Jaginne the elderly, women and children were left to take on much of the heavy physical work of farming to aid the few remaining men now responsible for meeting the practical needs of the village.

Hildegard had recently left school and Gretel brought the news that their teacher Mr Novak had been drafted into the Army. He was highly regarded and he entered as an Officer – a Lieutenant. Suddenly life had taken a very serious turn. As the younger men departed, a large black cloud of uncertainty descended upon Jaginne, and their happy, carefree days became a thing of the past.

Chapter 12

Convent Days

In Hitler's Germany, after leaving formal schooling at aged 14, it became a rule for all young women under the age of 25 to undertake a *Pflichtjahr* (duty year). Whilst the young men went to fight, the young women would partake in some kind of service, perhaps working on a farm or giving help to families with several children, or a year of extra schooling to improve their prospects in the future. This year of duty was compulsory.

Hildegard on leaving school, in the spring of 1939, decided that for her Pflichtjahr she would like to enrol at the nearby Convent as a weekly boarder to learn shorthand, typing and book keeping. The Convent School Cloister was located in Carlsruhe and she could easily cycle the distance at the beginning and end of the week.

The daily schedule at the Convent started at 5am when the duty year girls would rise and go straight to mass. From there they were assigned chores to be completed before breakfast. Hildegard's duties were in the kitchen which suited her very well.

The day-students who had enrolled for higher education arrived after breakfast and Hildegard would join them for the shorthand and typing lessons. The Pflichtjahr girls were required to help with cooking lunch and preparing tea for all the nuns and students.

Sleeping arrangements consisted of several small dormitories each housing six beds separated by modesty curtains. In each of the dormitories four students would sleep with two nuns. One evening whilst getting ready for bed one of the girls in the dormitory decided to peek through a gap in the curtain at a nun who was getting changed to see if she had any hair, only to have her suspicions confirmed. Her head had been completely shaved! Four girls sharing a dormitory was a recipe for excitement and

Hildegard enjoyed those times as she and three fellow Pflichtjahr girls prepared for bed, all chatting and laughing as they relaxed and shared funny stories of the day. Until they heard the nuns' approaching footsteps, at which point the fun stopped and they all quickly slipped under their *federbeds* (duvets) and pretended to be asleep.

During her time at the Convent Hildegard learned many cookery skills. The nuns baked bread each day and a rota was created for the Pflichtjahr boarders to take turns to rise extra early to help with the baking. Nuns and students alike all enjoyed the benefits of fresh bread every day. The girls would also bake biscuits. Chocolate biscuits and almond biscuits. Delicious treats in those frugal times. Hildegard would save left over biscuits in a tin to take home for her mother and Gretel at the weekend and she'd always set some aside to take as a gift to her father when visiting him in the nursing home.

Hildegard soon realised that her idea to spend a year at the Convent had been a very good one. She was learning practical skills as well as skills to help her find a good job, whilst at the same time meeting lots of new people and having plenty to eat and lots of fun. With the country at war, she was glad she had the distraction of her busy life at the Convent.

The Convent was a very happy place to be as all the girls were friendly and helpful towards one another. As well as enjoying her tasks and studies and friendships, Hildegard was able to appreciate the delightful surroundings in which the Convent was situated. The elegant grounds included a lake, many various and beautiful trees and well-kept flower and shrub gardens which were tended by the nuns. It was so pretty and peaceful one would never have guessed there was a war going on. She would often see a particularly gifted nun sitting at an easel painting stunning landscapes or the swans on the lake against a backdrop of trees. Hildegard could not think of a more wonderful and perfect place to live and work. She wished she could stay forever.

As she continued to enjoy her work in the kitchen, on the approach to Christmas one of the nuns demonstrated how to make *Pfeffer kuchen* (gingerbread). Hildegard watched with interest as a gingerbread house was created and, on her next trip home, she collected the necessary ingredients together and made one for her mother to serve to a friend she had invited to tea. Sheets of gingerbread were baked and cut and stuck together with icing to make the shape of a house. She added a roof to the top and stuck sweets all over. She surrounded the house with plenty of icing to resemble snow and added a little fence around the perimeter. She was very pleased with her creation.

In time Hildegard made a special friend at the Convent. Her name was Hilde Rust. Hilde lived much further afield so it was not so easy for her to go home at the weekends so Hildegard would occasionally invite Hilde to her house as Jaginne was only 4km away. On one occasion Hildegard planned a trip by train to Hilde's house taking Gretel with her for the outing. She was amazed at the size of Hilde's beautiful home. It was called *'Guten Tag'* ('Good Day') and the house was completely covered with a grapevine. Having seen little of life outside of her village, the trip was an exciting experience.

Other than Hilde's weekend visits, Hildegard also enjoyed meeting with her local friends. One Saturday evening she and her friends happily set off to a dance which had been arranged a short distance away in another village. Girls were used to dancing together as male dance partners were rare these days due to most being called to fight, so Hildegard was surprised to meet a young man who had attended her school. After explaining about her duty year at the Convent as a boarder, he told her he had recently turned 18 so had been called up to join the Army and would be leaving soon. He asked would she write to him. The young man's name was Georg (pronounced Gay-org) Ziegallr and Hildegard thought him very brave. Villagers were all encouraged to write to local soldiers to keep their spirits up and so it was agreed that he would write to her at the Convent and let her know where he was stationed so she could write back.

Back at the Convent one of Hildegard's friends had become a *Novizen-Nonne* (nun in training). Her name was Sopfie and she had been accepted to train as a novice. She had a nice new black habit with a tiny white collar. She looked very smart and she wore a small head covering which, unlike the ordained nuns, did not cover her hair. Hildegard and Hilde asked her "Why did you decide to become a nun? How do you like being a novice? What do you have to do?" So many questions but Sopfie was glad to tell the girls all they wanted to know and they were very impressed by what they heard. Sopfie's comment that in the Convent they'd be safe from the war was a very reassuring consideration for the two friends. Together with thoughts of the goodness of the nuns and the friendly girls – as well as the beautiful environment, Hilde Rust announced the next day that she wanted stay at the Convent and become a nun. She was very serious about it. Hildegard thought about this and, for the same reasons as her friend, she decided she wanted to do the same. The girls arranged that, during their visits home the following weekend, they would each tell their families of their intentions.

As planned, after lunch on the Saturday, Hildegard told her mother that she had decided to become a nun. "Hilde!!" exclaimed Mama. "No! You are only 15 and you are too lazy to become a nun. You have enough difficulty getting up early each morning as it is so I don't think you would like those early mornings every day for the rest of your life! And you wouldn't like to spend so much time on your knees. And do you really want to go to mass every day and become a missionary and go off to Africa and India and look after sick people?" Hildegard didn't know what to say. She didn't want to admit it but Mama was right. "And also", her mother continued, "I have had a letter from Matron at the Convent asking if I have knowledge that you write to a soldier, and to point out that the Convent does not allow the girls to have boyfriends or write to boys. I doubt very much that they would have you!" The nuns had intercepted a letter from Georg and opened it. Instead of reprimanding her, as Matron fully expected her to do, Maria suggested to her daughter that she should ask Georg to write to their home address. And so it was agreed that Hildegard was not suited to a life in the cloisters. Hilde Rust's parents also said no.

After several letters back and forth between Hildegard and Georg Ziegallr who was stationed at the Front, his parents wrote to tell her that sadly he would not be coming home. He had been shot and had died of his wounds. He was 19 years of age.

Chapter 13

The Effects of War and Starting Work

The war continued and on 10th May 1940 Winston Churchill became Britain's new Prime Minister.

One year after the start of the war, in September 1940, Hitler signed the Tripartite Pact between Nazi Germany, Fascist Italy and Imperial Japan to create an alliance between the three countries. Hungary, Romania and Slovakia, Bulgaria, Yugoslavia and Croatia, attracted by promised gains, also signed the Pact.

Immediately after the Tripartite Pact, and despite the signing of the Molotov-Ribbentrop Pact with the Soviet Union the year before, Hitler audaciously began planning an invasion of Russia.

As safe and beautiful as her environment was, Hildegard was unsettled by pieces of news being related by friends in the Convent. She had seen, even before the war started, that Jews were required to wear a mark on their sleeves. It was a blue Star of David embroidered onto a white armband. There were lots of Jews living in Carlsruhe and the town had a synagogue built there. On trips to Carlsruhe, her mother would buy fabric from a shop run by a Jewish family. It was cheap and Mama liked a bargain. The owners were very friendly and they greeted each other by name. There were several shops in the town that were run by Jews. One Sunday on their walk to church, they noticed that the synagogue had been burnt to the ground and all the gravestones had been knocked down and ruined. Her mother asked neighbours what had happened and she was told that all the Jews had disappeared. This didn't make any sense to Hildegard and her family. They could not imagine where they had all gone.

After her Pflichtjahr Hildegard decided that, even though she wasn't going to become a nun, she would like to stay another year at the Convent to continue her studies and pass the relevant exams. Her mother agreed, even though there was a fee to be paid. During this year, to save boarding fees, she lived at home and cycled to and from the Convent as a day-student without having to work in the kitchen or do any chores.

April 1941 and aged 16, Hildegard passed her exam in shorthand and typing and left the Convent. She very quickly found employment in the office at Carlsruhe Railway Station where her father had worked until his accident. Many of his colleagues still worked at the station so she was able to settle into the job very quickly. Her father had worked in the office managing the timetables and all the incoming and outgoing trains. Hildegard's position was based in the booking office selling tickets, giving information about connections and managing the accounts. Everyone at the station worked in shifts, either 5am - 2pm or 2pm - 10pm a week at a time and then change. Hildegard would cycle the 3km there and back. She had to ensure she was in bed very early when on the early shift as rising early was not easy for her. To get to the station on time she had to be out of bed by 3.30am, with Mama calling quietly "Get up! Get up!"

Her mother would be already out of bed and dressed and preparing Hildegard's breakfast to help her. She tried not to disturb Gretel who at 15 years of age had begun her Pflichtjahr in a local flour mill and was thankful that she didn't need to rise that early. Although she like her sister had left school at 14, Gretel had stayed at home for a year because her mother decided she was too thin and could be anaemic. The year enabled their Mama to build up her younger daughter in order to help her cope with the physical work at the mill.

The family had heard from Oncle Hans that their cousin Norbert's two older brothers, Rudi and Willi, had both been drafted into the *Wehrmacht* (Combined Armed Forces). Later news came that Rudi had been badly wounded and very sadly Willi had been killed in action.

Another sad announcement was made that, after serving in the war for one and a half years, Hildegard's teacher, Franz Novak, had been killed in action. Many young men from the village had been killed and Mr Novak's family was yet another casualty in this senseless war. The whole village knew Mr Novak and mourned his loss, no less the Scheitza family. They were heartbroken when they heard the news. He had been so kind to the girls in the absence of their father. He was a very good man. There was a church service for him which all the villagers attended.

Every passing day Hildegard, her friends and her family hoped the war would end. Each Sunday at church announcements were made of young men who had been killed or who were missing. So many tears were shed as many of her school friends had been lost.

Hildegard's late teenage years were far from how she had expected them to be but she and her friends were determined to occasionally create some fun for themselves whenever they could. Hildegard would invite friends to the house to play records on the gramophone in the arbour and try out different dances, and the music would transport them to a happy place where they could imagine the world was back to normal and at peace.

All the young men she knew had been drafted and Hildegard and her friends continued to write letters to them and make knitted sacks in which to send provisions. Whilst working at the railway station Hildegard was able to wish soldiers well as they headed off to meet their units, sadly not knowing who if any would survive and return. Much more enjoyable though was the opportunity to welcome home the soldiers who, after being away for many months, had finally been granted leave.

There was great excitement when families heard their sons were coming home, even for a short while. When enough soldiers were returning, the surrounding villages would organise a dance for them. On one such occasion Hildegard and her friends were elated beyond words as it was weeks and weeks since the last dance and they would be seeing many of their friends again. In preparation new clothes were sewn and shoes were bought with saved coupons. One particular dance was a few kilometres away in Damratsch. Gretel came too with her friends and some of the boys who weren't yet old enough to join the Forces. Some walked and others cycled and no one complained about the distance due to this rare opportunity to be in mixed company again and dance and dance.

Chapter 14

Hitler Invades Russia

On 22nd June 1941, despite his non-aggression pact with Russia, Hitler advanced his well-trained and well-equipped Wehrmacht into the Soviet Union, code name Operation Barbarossa. The main aims were to eliminate the Communist threat to Germany and seize the western lands for German settlement. The western territories of Russia were rich in natural resources which would benefit Germany and fulfil Hitler's plan to acquire more *Lebensraum* (living space).

Over 3million German troops and 650,000 from Allied Forces, were positioned along the 2,900km Front Line which stretched from the Baltic Sea to the north and the Black Sea to the south. Hitler expected to advance quickly, get the job done and retreat successfully. It was the largest invasion in Military history. Warning had come to Stalin early on but he thought it to be a hoax and carried on as usual. German troops destroyed the Soviet Air Force and many towns and captured hundreds of thousands of ill-prepared Soviet troops, sending them to concentration camps.

In addition to the Wehrmacht, arrangements were made for the deployment of the *Einsatzgruppen* (Paramilitary Death Squads) made up of SS personnel and police, also known as mobile killing units. They would follow behind the German troops into the newly occupied areas. Their task was to establish an intelligence network with the aim of identifying groups of people hostile to German rule in the east and infiltrate and dig out Communist party officials who were subsequently lined up and shot. Anyone who endangered the success of German rule on Soviet territory would be eliminated. Just as important to Hitler, was the task of the Death Squads which would enable him to carry out his "final solution" policy. This being the systematic annihilation of Jews in Europe.

During the months of the raid the German Death Squads murdered thousands of Jews, annihilating entire Jewish communities. They'd be dragged out of their homes and, if they weren't sent to concentration camps to die in portable gas chambers, they would be given a spade and made to dig their own graves before being shot. In September 1941 in Kiev over 33,000 Jews were slaughtered, the total count being in the region of 1million by the end of the battle.

Hitler's Army headed victoriously for Moscow but Stalin, though initially surprised, very quickly rallied his eastern troops to move westward with guns, tanks and aircraft to be made ready to fight, with the rousing announcement "From Red Square to the Battle Front!" Whilst Moscow began the efficient planning and carrying out of counter offensives, women were brought into munitions factories working day and night to produce all the equipment the military needed.

Then Russia was joined by their greatest ally – the Russian winter. As the end of the year approached, temperatures dropped. The Red Army were of course well prepared with skis and sleds and winter camouflage and their cavalry to fight on the ground. They were also well equipped with anti-aircraft weapons, whilst their skilled Airforce would scatter the Nazi's from their 2,900km Front.

Along with thick snowfall it was Russia's coldest winter in 140 years. German troops were far from prepared. Their clothing and equipment proved they were no match for the Soviets together with the below freezing temperatures. Planning for swift victory over Russia, German troops had moved so fast they had outpaced their supply units. 3million Germans were captured, most were suffering from frostbite, and many were dying of the cold and starvation. It was a losing battle for Germany but the order never came to retreat. The fighting continued until 5th December 1941 when the Soviets launched a major counterattack which drove the Germans back from Moscow in chaos.

Germany's war with Russia caused some of the largest battles of WWII, and would be the cause of the most horrific atrocities and highest number of casualties on both sides.

Part Four

1942 - 1943

Chapter 15

Oppeln Station and Meeting Karl

Early in 1942, Hildegard was transferred from Carlsruhe to Oppeln (now known as Opole) Station. Oppeln was a large and important city in the region of Upper Silesia and it took her almost 2 hours to cycle the 35km from her home. Oppeln Railway Station had many more lines with trains coming and going in every direction to and from the larger towns and cities. The shifts were different as well. 6am - 2pm and 2pm - 10pm. There was also a night shift, 10pm - 6am. The fastest route to work was through the forest, and Hildegard was not coping with cycling in the dark as the forest was so dense it became pitch black. She was more than happy to cycle through in the daylight but the evening and night shifts were potentially dangerous. As she cycled, very fast, she would pass many wild-boar, all standing very still and following her with their eyes. She was petrified. The intense relief when she approached the edge of the forest and she could see moonlight was huge. This could not go on. Her nerves couldn't take it, so she decided to look for accommodation nearer to the station. She eventually found a nice lady in Oppeln who had a room to rent, a mere 100m walk away from her place of work which would be ideal for her. She now only needed to cycle between the station and home either side of her days off.

Life in Germany, even in remote villages, was drastically changing. Hitler had taken all the young men to fight and Nazi propaganda was now plastered on every fence and wall. As people became more aware of atrocities and the senselessness of the war, the Dictatorship was being viewed less and less favourably by many Germans. Hildegard's uncle in Berlin had told Maria not to believe the things Hitler was shouting about. Oncle Hans had very strong opinions which he shared very quietly, lest he 'disappeared'. If a man or woman went into a bar and said something detrimental about Hitler, that person would be seen no more. 'Disappearing' usually meant that dissenters would be taken to a concentration camp to be tortured and then, depending on the level of their crimes, would be either sent to a work camp or they would be shot. Maria was very nervous for Hildegard's safety at this larger station as she talked to many travellers. She would remind her daughter numerous times, and very clearly warned her "Hilde, do not say anything!"

Hildegard was enjoying her new job. She loved the hustle and bustle with many passengers constantly passing through, many of the travellers being soldiers heading to or from the Front. Hildegard was curious about the large number of Jewish people, easily identified by their Star of David badges, all heading east into Poland. They included male and female civilians of all ages, with entire families of parents and children and grandparents. Each carried a suitcase as if going away for a while. When discussions took place during a break, a colleague told her she'd heard they had been told of new jobs and new lives over the border. Knowing that Jews were being given a very hard time in Germany, she felt glad they were getting out of the country and were on their way to somewhere much safer, and she would wish them a safe journey as they passed through the ticket office.

With hundreds of Military personnel travelling through Oppeln Station every day Hildegard, at her post in the ticket office, felt it important to send the soldiers off to fight with a friendly and encouraging word as, although most seemed carefree as they joked and laughed together, some faces showed nervousness and fear of what might happen to them on the battlefield. Each of them had no idea what to expect other than they had no choice but to face the uncertain and probably difficult days ahead.

During one morning shift, whilst chatting to a soldier who needed to wait an hour for his train, a colleague arrived to take over Hildegard's post as it was time for her break. As she left the confines of the office the soldier seemed keen to continue the conversation and asked if she'd like to take a short walk along the station platform with him while he waited for his connection. Hildegard agreed and they walked and chatted. She learned that his name was Karl and he was on his way to the Front but could not say where. She found him very nice and friendly. He told her that he had no family to write to him and wondered if she would be happy to send him the occasional letter. Even though she knew nothing about him, she agreed. Then Hildegard's break was over and he boarded his train. On arriving home later that day she told her sister about the soldier. Gretel categorically told her "He won't write".

Hildegard dismissed her sister's negativity and sent a letter to Karl at the address he had jotted on a scrap of paper. She gave him her home address in the hope he would reply, and a little while later she received a letter from him. These were the first letters of many. He wrote well in *Kurrentschrift* (cursive script), a flamboyant script dating back several centuries which was not generally taught in schools at that time. Even though they had met on just one occasion, Karl said he missed Hildegard. A relationship began to grow through the letters but she had completely forgotten how he looked. All she could remember was that he had an unusual accent as he came from Stuttgart and spoke with the dialect of that area. Eventually he sent a photo and she in turn sent one back in return. The letters bore no mention of the war as that was strictly prohibited so she was completely unaware of where he was writing from. All incoming and outgoing letters were checked by the Military. Hildegard couldn't mention any news she had heard on the radio or read in the newspaper. Everything was secret. They just wrote about themselves and their lives before the war.

Hildegard learned that Friedrich Karl Wilhelm Bantel was born in Stuttgart on 4th October 1919, 5 years her senior. His mother wasn't married and could not look after her baby alone so she took him along to an orphanage where he was brought up and taught by nuns. It was during his schooling at the orphanage that the nuns taught him to write in the cursive script. Karl never knew his father and during his time at the orphanage his mother, who could have visited him, chose not to. There was never any communication, not even a birthday card. The little boy grew up thinking both of his parents were dead. Despite his unfortunate situation, Karl had a happy childhood and was well cared for by the nuns. The other orphans were like brothers and sisters to him and the orphanage was his home. He remembered playing lots of sports as he had many playmates in his large 'family'. Whilst he was still very young a couple wanted to adopt him but, when approached by the orphanage, his mother refused to give the permission needed as she planned to bring him home when he was of an age to earn money. At the age of 13 his mother, true to her word, came to collect him and took him to her home. She had married and Karl found he had 3 younger half siblings. His mother arranged a job for him in a factory. She would visit the factory each week on payday where he handed over his pay to her and she gave him a little spending money. Evenings and weekends his mother and her husband would leave Karl with the younger children while they went out drinking in nearby bars. At the age of 15 he was so tired of being used by his mother that he found a job earning more money in an iron foundry and he moved out. As soon as he was 16, in 1935, he joined the German Army.

Hildegard had no idea where Karl was stationed but she enjoyed hearing from him, knowing he was safe. Some time and several letters after meeting, in the summer of 1942, Karl was granted 2 weeks leave from his service in Poland. He intended to visit his uncle, his mother's brother, in Stuttgart who was a musician in a band, and his younger half-brother who he had stayed in touch with and was not yet old enough to join the Army. He did not want to see his mother to whom he never spoke again.

Karl wrote to Hildegard to ask if he could come and stay for a few days as he had been given leave. She asked her mother who agreed to the request and said he could stay in their best room.

On the morning of his visit, due to Hildegard's unclear instructions, Karl found himself at Konstadt Station. He asked the station master how far it was to the village of Jaginne and he was told it was 30km away. There was not much sign of life so he asked if there was any transport he could take. The station master said he was doubtful but he then noticed an elderly postman collecting mail from one of the carriages and he suggested Karl might ask if he could take him on his horse and cart. Karl, who had brought various drinks in his rucksack as gifts, offered him a bottle of whisky in payment for taking him towards Jaginne. The postman readily agreed as he was going in that direction anyway. It was a bumpy ride and Karl had to be taken even more kilometres out of his way as the postman dropped off bundles of mail to many Post Offices in various villages along the way. As Karl had a further, already opened, bottle of whisky in his rucksack, he and the postman would partake of an occasional drink to help refresh them on this long and winding journey.

There were very few cars in general use as most had been taken off the road for the war effort and Karl was very grateful to the postman. In Jaginne, there was one car and this belonged to the grocer. It was actually more of a truck than a car. The villagers' only means of transport was by bicycle or if they owned a horse and cart or, if they were very fortunate, the grocer might agree to take them where they needed to go in his truck.

Karl and the postman finally arrived in Jaginne. Hildegard had given up that he might arrive that day but suddenly her friend Anna Rosa came running to the house saying "Hilde, your boyfriend is coming!" Anna's parents ran the local Post Office and she and her sister helped deliver the mail as their brothers were away fighting in the war. On arrival at the Post Office with his passenger, the postman explained where the stranger was heading and Anna immediately ran ahead to alert Hildegard!

As soon as Hildegard heard the news, she suddenly had a bad attack of nerves and ran upstairs so when Karl finally arrived, she was hiding in the loft room. Gretel said "Go downstairs and see him, Silly!" Hildegard eventually plucked up the courage to slowly make her way down the stairs and sheepishly say hello to Karl and introduce him to her mother and Gretel. He had brought two bottles of advocaat as gifts. Hildegard remembered observing how polite he was. He was also funny and talked a lot and her family quickly warmed to him. There was much excitement as they welcomed this stranger into their home.

With her father still absent there were plenty of jobs needing to be done inside and outside of the home and Karl set about dealing with some repairs in the garden including mending the fence and the chicken run which pleased Hildegard's mother. The family found Karl to be charming and they all liked him very much, despite sometimes having trouble understanding his strong

Stuttgart accent. The young man was very friendly and her mother was so impressed by him that she agreed he could stay for the entirety of his two remaining weeks of leave and that Hildegard could throw a party for him and invite her friends and cousins and her sister's friends as well. Hildegard set about organising the party immediately. Invitations for a gathering of friends the next evening were delivered and a villager who played the accordion was also invited. With tasty food prepared by her mother and the advocaat brought by Karl, Hildegard was really happy that the party was a great success. For a few hours that evening friends and family forgot all about their troubles and danced away the evening on the veranda.

During Karl's stay the couple took walks and visited the cinema in Carlsruhe. As his time in Jaginne drew to a close Karl said that he couldn't promise Hildegard anything at this time but hoped that he would return in good health and in one piece from the war. He wanted to stay in contact with her. On his final night they celebrated again on the veranda with village friends.

All too soon it was time for Karl to leave and return to his Army base and then leave for the Front. The time together had given the two young people the opportunity to get to know each other a little more. As trust between them grew, they had carefully talked about Hitler and the war and Karl shared with Hildegard his thoughts on the Nazi regime and the brainwashing and some of the bad and crazy beliefs and ideas he did not hold with.

Gretel accompanied Hildegard and Karl to the station. Tears filled Hildegard's eyes as she wondered if she would ever see him again. Neither knew long the fighting would continue but they were grateful for this time together and hoped that the war would finally come to an end and they would meet again.

There was nothing Hildegard could do but pray for Karl's safety and remain busy with her job and providing help to her mother, whilst hoping that one day she would see him again. Gretel, who was now working in a kindergarten, was a great friend and companion, as well as a sweet sister, and the two girls spent their free time together with visits to Carlsruhe with its shops and cinema.

Chapter 16

The Battle of Stalingrad

22nd August 1942 began what was to become the bloodiest and deadliest battle of the World War II. Unperturbed by his massive defeat at Moscow just a few months before, Hitler was now ready for his second plan to take land and resources from, this time, Stalingrad (now known as St Petersburg). Firstly, the oil fields of the Caucasus region were bountiful and Germany was running short of oil due to the war. Secondly Stalingrad, alongside the River Volga, had built a huge manufacturing industry. The region was famous for its fertile agricultural fields and Germany was short of food. Hitler claimed it would be the 'bread basket of Germany'.

Led by the newly appointed General Paulus, the first advance by Hitler's highly decorated 6th Army, with orders to kill at will and capture the city, was successful. But Stalin was so determined to defend this city, so named in his honour, that he mobilised every soldier and civilian. Severe bombing by the Luftwaffe left the city in ruins which was followed by months of bitter street fighting.

By mid-November the Soviets had encircled the Germany Army, 200,000 men, in the centre of the city. December and January saw temperatures drop to below zero and German troops, if they were not killed in the fighting, were being slowly starved or frozen to death. After fierce fighting in dreadful conditions, on 2nd February 1943, the remaining 91,000 German soldiers surrendered and were taken to Soviet prison and labour camps. 91,000 of which, a decade after the war, less than 6,000 returned to their homeland.

The defeat at Stalingrad was one of the biggest turning points of the war, with 2million dead and enormous numbers of casualties on both sides.

Chapter 17

Karl is Shot

Having not heard from Karl for many weeks, in the spring of 1943 Hildegard finally received a letter from him telling her he had been shot through his shoulder. Germany had been defeated at Stalingrad with mammoth deaths and injuries on both sides. Karl had found his way to a field hospital before being transported to a Military hospital in *Oberschreiberhau* (now Szkarska Poreba). The Riesengebirge Hotel had been converted into a hospital for wounded soldiers and was a 5-hour train journey away from Jaginne.

Hildegard when asking her mother if she could visit Karl, received a very firm "No!" in reply but, seeing the tears in her daughter's eyes, Maria softened and eventually agreed she could go, saying "But you are not going anywhere without Gretel!

Oberschreiberhau was located in the *Karkonosze* or Great Mountains so there would be snow on the ground, even in springtime. The sisters, dressed in their light brown astrakhan coats, fur hats, fur gloves and boots, set off for the station at the crack of dawn as the train journey would take at least 5 hours. Hildegard, due to her job at Oppeln Railway Station, was granted free travel so only Gretel's ticket needed to be paid for.

Finally arriving at their destination, they were glad of their warm clothes as, despite the sunshine, it was very cold. As they stepped out of the station to begin the walk to the hospital, they were awestruck by the breathtaking views of glistening snowcapped mountains as far as their eyes could see. It was a beautiful sight.

By the time they arrived at the very grand and imposing building which now served as a hospital, Hildegard had begun to lose confidence and felt nervous. Would she even recognise him? The porter asked which patient they were visiting and asked the young ladies to take a seat. It wasn't long before Karl arrived in the lobby and with much relief she could see he looked exactly the same, though somewhat thinner. Hildegard's nerves soon evaporated as she realised what he had been through and the terrible pain he had suffered. His arm was being supported by a brace and the empty sleeve of his jacket hung limply down by his side. Karl laughed when he saw the sisters and called them the two teddy bears due to their being dressed from head to toe in fur.

The girls had brought Karl gifts of a pair of gloves, a scarf and some sausage, bread and cake, all of which he accepted gratefully. Hildegard had wondered what the hospital would be like but she was glad to note that it was bright and clean. It was one of the many large and prestigious hotels that had been converted into Military hospitals and she was pleased that Karl was being well looked after in such pleasant surroundings.

As the three sat and chatted over coffee, Karl recounted how his unit had been fighting in Russia. It was a bitterly cold winter with deep snowfall and below freezing temperatures. Although they believed they were well-armed and well-trained, German troops had not been provided with adequate clothing or equipment for the harsh winters of Eastern Europe. Many had become hindered by frostbite. Food supplies were unable to get through the icy conditions and soldiers were starving as well as frozen. The Russian Army therefore had no problem driving them back into Poland.

Karl told Hildegard and Gretel how his unit had come under intense fire and he took a shot to his shoulder. There was no one left alive around him and there was no medical help. He had no choice but to lay very still in the freezing snow and wait until the coast was clear to crawl to a place of shelter until nightfall. Although in great pain, Karl was determined to walk throughout the night to prevent being discovered. There were many deserted houses and buildings he could use as cover along the way and he needed to keep moving as far west as possible, away from the Soviets.

Karl explained that as soon as the sun began to rise, he searched for an empty building in which to hide and sleep during the daylight hours. He did not know how he found the strength that night to walk again for miles in such terrible pain, until he reached the border into Germany. His shoulder wound had clearly become badly infected and the pain was even more acute. Once across the border he felt it safe to flag down an oncoming truck. The driver, an elderly man, agreed to take him to the nearest field hospital where at last his wound could be treated. Karl counted his blessings for, if caught, he'd have been sent to a forced slave labour camp in Siberia. In contrast however, he was sent to the very nice hospital in Obershreiberhau to fully recover. It was from here that he was able to write to Hildegard.

Both Hildegard and Gretel were shocked by Karl's story as they had heard very few details of the battles their troops were having to endure. All news was under the total control of the regime and heavily propagandised, keeping the German population largely unaware of the facts but rather convincing them that all the fighting and loss of life was necessary for the good of Germany, to encourage continued national pride. It opened the sisters' eyes to the very real horrors of war.

Karl took the sisters to the Officers' Mess to have coffee and some food. He said they could stay overnight as there were guest rooms available but they had promised their mother they would return home that evening. Meanwhile they were able to enjoy the Officers' Mess where a tea dance was in full swing with lovely music. It was good to see the mostly wounded service men having fun and enjoying themselves whilst recovering from all kinds of physical and mental trauma suffered in battle.

The time flew by and the girls needed to say goodbye and face the long journey home. Before they left, Hildegard and Karl promised to continue to write to each other and as they were saying their goodbyes all three cried as they wondered whether or not the couple would ever have the chance to meet again.

Several weeks later Karl sent a letter saying that he was being posted to Italy which Hildegard read with relief. She was so glad he was not being sent back again to Russia. The couple continued to write to each other regularly over a period of several months, with a later communication stating that he had been posted to Holland. This was in fact the last of the letters between Karl and

Hildegard for some time, due to all telecommunications being shut down. For the next two years there was no contact.

The war raged on and as well as causing the loss of millions of lives, civilians continued to struggle due to the state of the economy. The Government continued to provide each citizen with coupons for food and necessities which helped a little. Civilians were means tested so, due to the pig Hildegard's family reared each year, coupons for meat were deducted. Thankfully the family had their vegetable plot and the neighbours looked after each other by sharing as much as they could. The Scheitza's goat gave them milk and they were able to produce a little butter for themselves. They continued to pick fruit in the forest but it was more difficult to sell so they used the fruit to barter for other items they needed like bread. Maria was able to make cakes and buns and potato dumplings thanks to their potato harvest. Living in a farming community was a blessing as they were better off than most, and living far away from major towns and cities meant they felt relatively safe.

Part Five

1943 – 1945

Chapter 18

Stalingrad Defeat, Germany Loses its Grip

Although he would not admit defeat, the annihilation of a huge part of the German army at the Battle of Stalingrad in February 1943 had been the beginning of the end for Hitler. The Allies had demanded unconditional surrender when troops were surrounded with no way out and Hitler was outraged. No committed Nazi General should ever surrender as that would mean the end of the Nazi regime. It was victory or death. Continue to fight and never give up. If everyone is going to die anyway the important action is to do the honourable thing! However, Field Marshall Paulus, to Hitler's disgust, put the troops' well-being first, something that had never been done before under Hitler's leadership.

Military and civilians alike were sick of the war. Germans as a whole, due to the relentless propaganda, had been completely indoctrinated to the point of abject loyalty to their leader, but many were beginning to lose heart.

Despite victory at Stalingrad, Stalin was incandescent at Hitler's massive invasion of his country which had caused so much carnage and destruction with a death toll of over a million. He was furious that he had been duped by the German leader's so called 'peace pact'. Retribution would be in the form of counter attacks by the Red Army as they moved westwards ridding Russia of all remaining German troops, reclaiming their lands and moving further west into Germany, the focal point being Berlin.

At the same time, on 18th February 1943, to combat confusion and discontent amongst the Military and the people alike, Joseph Goebbels had given a speech at the Berlin Sportspalast in front of a hand-picked 14,000 strong audience of fanatical Nazis. The long and manically nationalistic speech was to encourage the country and to counter Nazi Germany losing its grip on the war. At the end of his speech Goebbels whipped his audience into a patriotic frenzy. "Do you want total war? Yes or No?" echoed loudly through the hall. "Yes! Yes!" came the equally loud and even more stirring and patriotic reply. The speech was broadcast and heard on the radio by Military and civilians alike so the propaganda would spread and therefore affect the German population and promote stronger loyalty to the Fuhrer and the Nazi regime.

The war continued with Russia, now Hitler's greatest enemy, taking back territories and pushing back westwards from the Eastern Front.

In June 1944 the Western Allied Armies landed at Normandy in France and began to drive the Germans back towards Berlin, showing their dominance from the west. Italy had fallen and Hitler and the German Army continued to struggle despite Goebbels' 'Total War' speech.

In addition to being attacked from both sides, from the summer of 1944 German cities were being fiercely attacked from above and flattened by aerial bombardments. However, in the midst of the devastation, Germany's system of bureaucracy had recovered its efficiency and, with proficient systems in place, life somehow went on.

On 20th July 1944 an assassination attempt, code named Operation Valkerie, was made on Hitler's life which was hoped to result in a coup leading to the end of the fighting. At the start of a conference a suitcase filled with explosives was placed close to Hitler but one of his aides inadvertently moved it slightly resulting in six staff members being killed by the blast with Hitler surviving completely unscathed. The perpetrators were arrested and executed.

After this Hitler decided to keep a lower profile and, whilst doing so, he carried out a purge on his High Command. All sceptics were replaced by hardliners who were prepared to fight till the bitter end.

In August 1944 the city of Breslau (now Wroclaw), situated 70km from Jaginne was declared by Adolf Hitler to be one of four *Festung* (Fortress) towns he was henceforth organising along Germany's eastern territories to protect the country from expected further onslaught by Russia. These fortress towns, with

Breslau the largest by far, were to be defended at all costs. The command to every civilian in the area and the Military was to create lines of defence. And so began the work of knocking down buildings, digging out trenches and building walls to act as barricades. Breslau's city centre was largely demolished to become an airstrip. On no account should the Red Army be permitted access. Hitler was determined that the enemy should not infiltrate Germany from the east.

October 1944 saw Soviet troops seriously begin their assault into East German territories. East Prussia, to the north, was the location for their first infiltration onto German soil. Battle commenced with the German Wehrmacht in defence against the Red Army with German troops successfully driving out the Russians. After the battle, the Red Army continued westwards to the rural town of Nemmersdorf (now part of Russia and known as Mayakovskoye). 48 hours after that fateful 'visit' a most shocking scene was discovered by German troops. A discovery that would put fear into every German civilian's heart. German field police reported the results of the most atrocious attack on the women, children and elderly of the village; all except one, who lived to report the unspeakable atrocities of that day. Reports vary as to the total number of civilians who were killed on that day but after suffering horrific torture and rape, each had been shot dead at point blank range. As well as the civilians, 50 prisoners of war who had been given the task of tending horses nearby, were also slaughtered.

On hearing of this, Hitler's immediate decision was to put his propaganda machine to work and he instructed Goebbels to send out information of the attack to citizens living in the easternmost towns and villages of Germany. The strong message in the propaganda was to warn citizens not to run, even though the Russian Army was on the offensive and killing civilians, but to demand they stay and fight. The propaganda, meant to anger citizens into battle mode, showed photos of the dead and stated that most of the town of 653 civilians had been killed, the numbers having been embellished by Goebbels for greater effect.

Nemmersdorf was just the beginning of thousands of Soviet atrocities carried out on German civilians. The extent of Russian hatred for Nazis for the deaths and destruction of their people and their country, spread to the entire German population and in their eyes all Germans should be punished. As Hitler used the hideous story of the massacre at Nemmersdorf as propaganda, more and more German civilians began to see the regime was not taking any account of the protection of the people. In the light of this and his now near depleted Army, Hitler ordered a new national Militia to be established. He called it the *Volkssturm* (People's Storm, otherwise known as the People's Army).

Due to the fact that all males from the age of 18 upwards had already been conscripted, the Volkssturm comprised all healthy, unconscripted males from 16 to 60. These included those serving in the Home Guard, many of whom had previously served in the Great War and who were initially considered too old to fight or who had been wounded. Also called to join were boys belonging to Hitler Youth who were too young to be sent to the Front but believed that to serve was an honour and a duty. Many women also joined the force. Even younger boys were required to run errands and deliver messages and supplies. Having been fired up by the recently reported Red Army atrocities, there became a renewed and fierce loyalty towards the Fuhrer and many were keen to enrol. Patriotic civilians were convinced that everyone should make sacrifices for the sake of Germany. Newly consigned members of the People's Army numbered 60,000 in the Berlin area alone. Very few uniforms were available so they wore their civilian clothes with a swastika armband. Members were provided with whatever weapons were readily available and briefly shown how to use them. Old men were taught to use powerful Punzas and were told that they were to fight till they were right down to the very last bullet. Very little training or preparation was given. Quantity, not quality, was required.

Meanwhile as British, French and American troops began to take occupation of West Germany, the Soviets, after their attacks on East Prussia, continued south in their mission to take control of town after town along East Germany's border. Men would be shot and women and girls raped. This boosted the call to the armies of the Reich, and also civilians, to fight for heart and home. Although the majority of members of the Military were totalitarian and fiercely loyal, some had had enough. However, any found complaining could expect harsh repercussions and desertion meant death. Marshalls scaled the country for deserters and would carry out executions by hanging. A 'drop out' soldier was one who had lost their unit and wandered around aimlessly trying to find it. Some faked being a drop out but to be found out meant death.

Chapter 19

Hitler Retreats to His Bunker

Between July 1944 and May 1945 more German civilians died than in any other time in the war. Most aerial raids over Germany happened after July 1944. Half of all Military losses were suffered in these final 10 months of the war. The longer war dragged on the more insane it got. The levels of destruction and human suffering were immense. 5.3million men of the 18.2million German Military were killed over the course of the war, mostly towards the end. At this point in time most German citizens were keen to keep their head down and prayed that there wouldn't be a bomb dropped on them and also that the American or British Military would come and liberate them.

Hitler was resolutely stubborn. Despite the appalling number of lives lost, there was no chance that he would surrender. He was determined to fight till the bitter end. He did not want to suffer the same disgrace of 1918, regardless of the human suffering it would incur. His rigidity caused him to exclude any other option. He was Supreme Commander of all Armed Forces. He was not giving up.

Several attempts had by now been made on the Fuhrer's life. After arresting and executing all perpetrators and sacking many of his Generals, on 16th January 1945 Adolf Hitler finally retreated to his exclusive and fully equipped *Fuhrerbunker* with his most senior staff. The bunker was situated 55 feet under the Chancery in Berlin. Although clearly unnerved, his delusional state caused him to believe that victory could still be his

From his bunker, in the same month, aware of the Soviets' serious attacks on Prussia and their aim to take more eastern territories, Hitler sent word to his Battle Commander, Karl Hanke, that all women and children were to be evacuated from Breslau to facilitate the city becoming a strong fortress town against Russian invasion. Following the Fuhrer's orders 100,000 civilians, including the elderly, were forced to leave in the middle of the night in the extreme cold, pulling prams, sledges and carts laden with all the belongings they could manage, along icy roads in the direction of Dresden. It was a punishing and unimaginably difficult journey as they battled through snowdrifts, slipping and sliding through the snow. It was cruel and heartless. Many babies and children died from the bitter cold and had to be left in ditches by their distraught mothers. Many of the weak knew they wouldn't make it so headed back to whatever fate might befall them in what had been their home town. Meanwhile, with Breslau's population gone, troops in the fortress town continued to build their defensive.

By the end of January 1945, the first bombs were dropped on Breslau and Soviets began to advance into the city.

Chapter 20

The Big Three Reorganise

Even before Hitler's retreat to his bunker, the Big Three powers had begun to devise plans for the Denazification of Germany and Allied Forces began searching for concentration camps. Germany had imprisoned thousands of prisoners of war in camps, with thousands left to die of starvation. On discovery of the camps, high ranking leaders such as Dwight Eisenhower, Supreme Commander of the Allied Expeditionary Force, visited the camps and were so appalled by the condition of the prisoners he demanded that all Nazis involved must be publicised, shamed and punished. Ordinary brainwashed Germans were gathered to see and confront what the Nazi regime had done. The intention of the Allies was to ensure this never happened again.

Even worse than the prisoner of war camps were the extermination camps. Despite attempts to keep Russian troops out of the camp at Auschwitz Birkenau, on 27th January 1945 it was finally liberated by the Red Army. Thousands of bodies were discovered, mostly innocent Jews who had been put to death in gas chambers. A sight such as this had never before been seen. The depths of depravity and inhumanity to man to which the regime had sunk was beyond belief. Allied personnel were brought in to assess the deplorable situation to try and reveal names of both perpetrators and the dead. It had been a murder machine created to consciously exterminate millions of innocent people of the Jewish race. Crimes that Germans and the world would never be allowed to forget. There could be no more turning a blind eye.

The Allies realised the entire German people needed a complete change of mind-set to undo years of Nazi indoctrination and demonstrate that almost every rule they had been living by was wrong. An enormous task lay before them. This was a huge challenge to Allied Military occupation.

With Germany on the brink of defeat and following the discovery of the concentration and death camps, the Big Three powers of the UK, USA and Russia, the heads of Government being Churchill, Roosevelt and Stalin, met at Yalta in the Crimean region of the USSR on 4th February 1945. Items on the agenda included discussions on reparations and the demilitarisation of Germany, with the most pressing item being the need to come to an agreement on occupation. The French President, General Charles de Gaulle was also present at the conference, and with the aim of re-establishing the nations of war-torn Europe, it was agreed that Britain would occupy the north western states, France the west and America the south. This would leave Russia with the entire stretch of eastern territories, the most eastern of which to be granted back to or gifted as reparations to the damaged Russia, Poland and Czechoslovakia. The populations of these countries would be organised so as to contain only the ethnic population of each of those countries.

Berlin would be occupied by all 4 countries. Similarly, it was agreed that the UK would control the north west of Berlin, France the west and the US the south west, with Russia occupying the entire easternmost areas of the city.

The reason for the planned strict separation of ethnicities, was due to the fact that *Volksdeutsche* (ethnic Germans) living in the eastern territories which had been formerly claimed by Germany, were now considered dangerous by non-Germans. Hitler was so hated by the peoples of the surrounding nations for the death and destruction he had waged over them, and that hatred now encompassed the entire German population. Volksdeutsche living in the once-German territories were now all suspected Fifth Columnists. They were closely watched as their presence in those countries presented a constant threat of uprisings to overthrow their governments. This was true of some but most were ordinary German people finding themselves now in a foreign country and the target of mistreatment, abuse and often violence or death. At the very least, ethnic Germans would have their jobs taken away from them so they couldn't look after themselves or their families. The Big Three agreed that as long as Germans were living in the reclaimed territories that there would always be a risk of another war.

Despite Hitler's command the previous year to ethnic Germans to stay where they were and lay claim to their land, most had no choice but to leave for fear of what would happen to them if they remained. They were effectively being forced out of what they considered to be their homeland. The Big Three realised that a massive operation lay ahead, and there was a need to somehow manage the expulsions. But the task was too enormous for any efficient plan to be announced, let alone one that would actually work.

So-called 'wild expulsions' had already begun to happen out of East Prussia, to the north, due to the Nemmersdorf Massacre. Ethnic Germans living in the north east were becoming aware that the Red Army intended to drive them out and they didn't want to wait for that day. The unsupervised expulsions resulted in many deaths. During those cold winter months even the able bodied were freezing to death or dying of starvation on their flights westward. The elderly and infirm did not stand a chance. The threat of abuse and mistreatment by the vengeful Red Army caused great fear amongst the refugees, adding even more distress to their unexpected predicaments.

Russian troops began to move along the north-eastern territories of Germany, occupying towns and villages east of the Oder Neisse Line and terrifying the townspeople. The decision made at the Yalta Conference had no set rules and, as the Red Army had no scruples in their treatment of the German people, many Volksdeutsche decided to be one step ahead and quickly packed belongings and fled. As previously out of Breslau the month before, the evacuations were taking place in the middle of the cold winter. Families were packing carts and dragging them through the snow. Mothers struggling with young children and prams with no husband to help them. Farmers driving trucks full of belongings, many of which would break down. Trains were full to bursting with refugees hoping to get to safety. On arrival in German towns and cities, many dead bodies would be found in railway carriages; mostly being the elderly and frail unable to survive the freezing temperatures. These were piled onto the platforms. Hundreds of them every day as Volksdeutsche desperately tried to get to Berlin or Dresden or other towns over the border into West Germany. The uncontrolled plan was bound to cause carnage.

The Big Three heads, on hearing of the 'wild expulsions', and the perilous plights of evacuees, realised something should be done. Their response was to demand that the Allies were to organise the situation and to 'enable and oversee' the evacuations.

Part Six

Early 1945

Chapter 21

Flight of the Volksdeutsche

Even though Nazi propaganda continued to tell another story to the German people, the end of World War II was in sight. The *Wehrmacht* (German Combined Forces) was in a state of collapse with many remaining units being trapped by the Red Army. Denazification of Germany was under way to remove Nazi perpetrators from power, to make arrests, and to dismantle and eradicate the Military. All annexed lands were to be returned. It was agreed that Poland was to be given back its occupied land and also 40,000 square miles of Germany's eastern territory.

Millions of ethnic Germans were now finding themselves in the 'wrong' place due to the Big Three's decision to 'cleanse' each country of alien ethnicities for the sake of future peace. And with reparations and return of lands, most of the German population living in the easternmost territories of Germany were in the process of losing their homes with entire communities forced to evacuate to the west.

On hand to 'enable' this enormous task of evacuation was the Red Army only too pleased to lay claim to German soil. The mass exodus of Volksdeutsche had already started in the north with Soviets brutally managing the movement. Fear of the Red Army, as they directed the lines of evacuees out of the east and towards the border, was justified due to their ruthless treatment of refugees which included women and girls being seized, taken away and raped. Many, especially the elderly, who were seen to be inadvertently putting a foot out of line or holding up the pace would be shot and left by the wayside. When Great Britain's Winston Churchill heard of the atrocities by Russian troops, he called for the expulsions to be carried out in an 'orderly and humane' manner. The message, however, did not seem to filter through.

Jaginne, the East German village in which Hildegard and her sister had grown up, was now becoming part of Poland. It was a huge shock for Hildegard and her family and neighbours when they heard they were to be evacuated out of Silesia. The land on which they currently stood and considered German soil now belonged to Poland and they were not welcome.

Neighbours in Jaginne and surrounding villages began to organise themselves for the evacuation. Norbert had already returned to his parents in Berlin leaving Hildegard, her mother and sister to pack their bags. Oppeln Station had arranged many trains to execute the move of all local ethnic Germans westwards. Villagers were being told when it was time for them to leave for the station. Everyone was on high alert, nervously awaiting instructions to leave.

In freezing temperatures, in the middle of the night on 11th February 1945 Hildegard, her mother and sister were jolted by a loud rap on the door. "Everybody out!" someone shouted. "The Soviets are 30km away and they are heading in this direction! With tanks!" This was enough to encourage speed to get out and get on the road for the two-hour walk to Oppeln Station. The Red Army's reputation of drinking too much vodka and their brutality was not something any of them wanted to experience.

Maria warmed coffee for each of them to take in flasks. They were allowed to take one bag per person on the train and enough food to last the day's journey. In preparation, Hildegard had laid out a thick coat to wear, packed another and decided to carry a further 'great coat' belonging to her father which she considered could be of use as a blanket. And now the time had come for the family to lock the door behind them and set off, wrapped in their warmest coats and boots with extra layers of clothing as protection against the sub-zero temperatures. Hildegard grabbed her bicycle and hung and balanced as much of their luggage as possible across the handlebars as she, her mother and Gretel joined the straggling line of neighbours all trudging through the snow in the direction of the station. Most hoped the evacuation would be a temporary measure and were convinced they'd be returning home, not fully understanding that this was part of a lasting agreement made by world leaders; a permanent scheme being put in place to ensure future peace.

Apart from those on foot there was a separate line leaving the village. These were the farmers who had decided to use their horse drawn carts and wagons to transport their families and belongings. Heavily weighed down by large trunks and animals and even furniture, they began their long trek through the snow to the west hoping they could stay clear of the Red Army.

The villagers walked in silence. No sound except for the crunch of snow beneath their feet as they made their way along the lanes away from Jaginne at early dawn, each bearing the weight of their luggage along with anxiety for their own and their families' immediate and long-term futures. Words were not necessary to convey the deep sadness, fear and concern felt by them all and encouragement was beyond them. Not one looked back as that would have been unbearable. Even those who had no choice but to leave loved ones behind as those without transport and who could not walk had to stay.

A message came through that the Soviets were closer than they thought. They were fast approaching. There was now no time to waste. They wanted to be as far ahead as possible. This huge transfer of people from one country to another was an enormous task. There was no possibility that the Red Army would carry it out in an orderly and humane way due to their quest for restitution. In their minds Germany should pay for its sins and all ethnic Germans should be treated like animals.

Chapter 22

The Train Journey

On reaching the railway station the villagers found fellow evacuees being directed onto trains as quickly as possible. They were told the trains were headed for Dresden, a day's train journey away. Hildegard didn't care where they were going as long it was far away from the clutches of the Red Army. She just hoped in her heart that one day, if the war ever ended and life returned to normal, that they might return to their homes.

An announcement was being repeated on a loud speaker that all railway employees were to wait and help out at the station before boarding a separate train later. They had also been informed that jobs may be found for them at other railway stations on arriving at their destinations. "Can I please take my mother and sister?" cried Hildegard to a station guard. "No! There's no room for relatives!" came the harsh reply. The three looked at each other. They were being separated and they had no choice but to obey the orders. They quickly hugged and kissed each other goodbye with Hildegard promising "I will find you when we reach Dresden! Write to Oncle Hans if we can't find each other!" Her mother and Gretel took hold of their luggage and made their way along the platform, quickly disappearing into the crowd of local villagers all urgently boarding the waiting train. As the train began to move, Hildegard found herself desperately peering into all the passing windows trying to catch sight of her dear Mama and sister but she couldn't see them. She stood alone as the train left the station until it was out of sight. As she prayed for her family's safety, she felt grateful they were heading away from danger and to safety.

Evacuees continued to arrive at the station from Oppeln and its many surrounding villages. Hildegard, 20 years of age and feeling bereft, realised that feeling sorry for herself wouldn't do.

She must pull herself together. She searched through the sea of concerned faces on the platform, some of whom were fellow railway employees, until she spotted a very familiar face. Elisabeth Scheitza was the daughter of her Oncle Franz, one of her father's brothers. Elisabeth told Hildegard how she had come on ahead of her family as they were too slow. The cousins shared shifts at Oppeln Station so they didn't see too much of each other as when one was working the other wasn't. Her mother preferred Hildegard not to mix with this particular relative due to her love for partying, but Hildegard liked her and she was glad they were to be travelling on this unfortunate journey together. But, in the meantime, there was work to do as the two girls were called upon to help people board onto the next waiting train.

With the arrival of daylight, the train for employees finally drew alongside the station platform and after heaving her bicycle into the luggage carriage Hildegard and Elisabeth quickly climbed aboard and very gratefully found two spaces on a bench seat. As the train began to move, both girls felt a sense of relief that they too were finally on their way. Away from the Red Army's advance. Heading, they hoped, to a place of safety where they would be reunited with friends and family.

Clutching her father's great coat to her for comfort, Hildegard watched sadly from the train window as Upper Silesia and the villages and the forest and her home disappeared into the distance. Trying to stay positive, she remembered with relief that Dresden was just a few hours away and she and her family would be together again before nightfall. Dresden was an obvious destination as although it was 350km (over 200 miles) away, a full day's journey by train, it was only a short distance over the new Polish/German border. She could only hope they would be able to find somewhere to stay.

After exchanging anxieties, thoughts and feelings with her cousin, Hildegard finally relaxed a little. The chugging of the train was somehow comforting as she looked through the window and watched the bleak February skies hanging gloomily over snow covered fields. Finally allowing herself to relax a little, she took stock of the situation, considering the past few desperate hours and the panic of packing and getting to the station in the middle of the night. Despite the initial relief and gratitude that she had Elisabeth to travel with, the reality of the situation caused fear. What would become of them? Tales of Red Army brutality came to her mind and she realised her safety was not guaranteed. Neither was that of her mother and sister. Such thoughts flashed in and out of her mind as her eyes stayed on the view from the window, the same view of snow-covered fields for mile upon mile. Hildegard prayed. She prayed that God would keep her mother and sister safe. She prayed for herself and Elisabeth and she prayed for all her colleagues on the train.

Due to the number of trains taking refugees out of eastern territories, the lines became clogged and the going was slow. Unfortunately, the train was forced to stop every few kilometres and would be motionless for long periods of time between stations to wait until the line cleared. Hour after hour passed by and they were clearly no nearer to Dresden. Thankfully the train stopped occasionally at other railway stations which enabled them to take the occasional short break when necessary. Hildegard wondered how her mother and sister were coping. They would of course be in the same situation, stopping and starting. She hoped they were comfortable enough and not too anxious. Poor Mama.

Hildegard's hopes of arriving in Dresden that evening had been well and truly quashed due to the unforeseen problems. Day turned into night and the passengers had no choice but to attempt to sleep. This turn of events had not been anticipated.

After a very uncomfortable night the next day was no different. The train moved a few kilometres before stopping again. Hildegard wished she hadn't eaten so much yesterday as there were only crumbs left from the food she'd packed for the journey and she was already beginning to feel hungry. Whilst daydreaming of her favourite food she felt a nudge in her ribs. It was Elisabeth offering Hildegard to share her last piece of bread. This she gratefully accepted whilst wishing she had left a little coffee in her flask to share. By lunchtime the girls felt sure they would be soon arriving in Dresden where they hoped to find hot food and drink.

The hours went by, mostly spent in a stationary position waiting for a clear line on which to continue. Once again night fell and they were still far from their destination. Sleeping on the train was difficult to say the least. Hildegard and Elisabeth had given up their seats long ago to those in need and were sitting on the floor. They were travelling third class and Hildegard imagined that the station bosses were travelling second class which would be much more comfortable. As a station employee she had been granted free second-class travel so she knew the difference. Father's great coat helped pad the floor a little and she was glad she'd brought that third coat for added warmth but it was not enough to prevent her limbs becoming stiff and sore and very cold. There was no food, no comfort, no heating and no light, all of which, during the long hours of darkness, caused extreme suffering, especially for the older passengers.

A third day on the train dawned and, again, renewed hope that by the end of this day they would arrive in Dresden and Hildegard would find her mother and sister. But the hours slowly passed in the same way. As the train was carrying only railway staff, there were no elderly and no children but even so all the passengers were exhausted and frozen. Some were suffering more than others from the harsh conditions and some began to fall ill. There was no food and only a little cold water to drink. The journey was never ending and increasingly uncomfortable and painful.

During the long hours spent on the train, railway colleagues would occasionally regale different pieces of information they had picked up from travellers passing through their stations. Some had heard of the treatment of Volksdeutsche in East European countries such as Serbia, Croatia, Romania and Hungary who were also being forced out of their homes. Those Germans were not being evacuated to the west and to safety but instead were being transported to work camps further east into Russia. For years they had been subjected to bad treatment by the ethnic populations of the countries in which their ancestors had lived, simply because they were ethnic Germans. Some partisans felt it their right to enter a German's home and take what they wanted. Some wanted to make life increasingly difficult for them. But now with the rule to evacuate, Volksdeutsche in East

European countries were experiencing something much worse. Suspecting every natural German to be a Fifth Columnist, the Red Army would arrive in a town or village, seek out all those of German blood and force them out of their homes as they were, confiscating anything of any value. If anyone tried to hide or escape, they were shot. One moment a mother would be bringing up her children alone whilst her husband had been called to fight at the Front, and the next she was manhandled out of her home and transported with her children to a living hell. The work camps were disgusting and the people were treated worse than animals. Old and young alike being bundled into trucks and forced to live in the worst and most frugal conditions.

Hearing such terrible news, Hildegard counted her blessings that she, her friends and family were not being made to suffer the fate of Siberian work camps as these other poor unfortunate souls were forced to do. She was so very glad they were heading in the right direction to the west.

A journalist writing of both the massive exodus west of thousands of ethnic Germans and of the abduction of further thousands into work camps said "Expellees were victims of a bad political decision" which was very true, to say the least.

En route at one of the railway stations it was announced that the fortress town of Breslau was under siege. Breslau was only 70km away from Jaginne. Hildegard had heard that much work had been carried out there to try and prevent the Soviets from continuing to gain occupation of the Eastern Territories. Hitler had ordered that on no account should the Russians be permitted entry and Breslau should be defended at any cost. With depleted troops he had called in the *Volkssturm*, his new makeshift Army, to help. He was determined that along with Berlin, this city would not be taken from him. The 1st Ukrainian Front had encircled the town, followed by the most terrible battle which marked the beginning of the siege.

This was bad news and brought home the danger to all her fellow countrymen living in the eastern territories. However, Hildegard decided to remain positive and be grateful for her safety and continued to pray that her family and friends were too, including those who had to stay due to age or infirmity.

Stories and rumours continued to be related on the train, some of which were far from helpful and just spread fear. One spoke of boys being pulled off trains by Russian soldiers to be sent to work camps, as well as stories regarding the terrible treatment of young women, those being well known. It seemed there was no crime too abhorrent for many members of the Red Army.

Tales were shared of the plight of evacuees in even more hazardous situations than Hildegard and her fellow travellers.

They were told of farmers, struggling along snow covered roads with their overloaded horse drawn carts, being shot for the crime of being too slow and holding up progress of a refugee convoy. Hildegard and her cousin thought of some of the farmers they knew and hoped that none had suffered this dreadful fate. Who on earth was in charge of these evacuations? Who if anyone is concerned for their safety? These dark and unnerving stories caused clouds of dread to be cast over them. To date Hildegard and her fellow villagers had been largely unaffected and even unaware of most of the tragedies of the war. Although all had suffered and mourned the devastating loss of many men and youths from their villages, the refugees' lives had not yet personally come face to face with danger or the enemy in this dreadful war. This journey was punishing enough without the fear of worse things happening to them along the way. Hildegard prayed. There was nothing else that could be done.

As the train slowly progressed, the travellers heard that excessively clogged lines into Dresden had caused decisions to be made to take a quicker and easier route to another town. Hildegard panicked at this news as she was now unsure if her mother and sister would be going in the same direction.

Chapter 23

The Bombing of Dresden

After the third mostly sleepless night on the train, at an early morning stop, news was filtering through that Dresden had suffered the most dreadful bombing raids all through the night and there was much destruction, leaving many dead. Shock spread through the carriages as people heard the news of how the British Airforce had carried out a major raid from the sky. Until now Dresden had been completely intact. The city had, in fact, become a safe haven for many evacuees, including thousands from the fortress town of Breslau. But war is no respecter of persons. Along with refugees, people from all walks of life and Military personnel in their thousands had perished.

Secondary shock waves came as people realised that if the train had moved at a normal pace they would have been settled in Dresden by now and would have also suffered that terrible fate. Hildegard immediately thought of her mother and sister but great relief came as colleagues calculated that their train had left only an hour or so beforehand and they too would still be caught up in the queues of trains trying to move. Hildegard hoped and prayed that this was the case. Dresden was now definitely discounted as their destination.

Clearly the war was far from over. When oh when will it end wondered Hildegard. The train with its even more shaken and weak passengers continued to stop and start throughout the entirety of this fourth day on the train, resulting in yet another painful night on the tracks.

The morning of the fifth day of this unbelievably long and excruciating journey, brought news that more air raids had been carried out over Dresden, this time by the American Airforce and that a total of 4 raids had been carried out all in all. Fire had spread throughout the city and Dresden was now lying in ashes with the loss of thousands of lives. The shocking total of deaths was almost 25,000.

Quite soon after hearing these horrifying stories the train, which had now crossed the border into Czechoslovakia, drew alongside a station platform and the passengers were greeted by a group of women serving bowls of soup. Visibly shaken, the weak, starved, sick and frozen evacuees climbed down from the train and queued for the most welcome meal of their lives. Those too weak to move had the food passed to them on the train. Never had hot soup, a wedge of bread and coffee tasted so good and never had it been so appreciated. The people of Czechoslovakia were obviously very kind.

Hildegard relished the feeling of the warm liquid as it began to thaw her body and felt the food giving her a little of the sustenance she desperately needed. She and Elisabeth even managed to exchange small smiles in their mutual comfort of this surprise blessing. As they stood on the platform clutching their mugs to warm their hands, she wondered where her mother and Gretel were and how they were being treated. Was this welcome repast only due to Hildegard being a railway employee? She hoped they were bearing up and that they too had also received a similar act of kindness. She hoped they were warm and that the end of their journey was in sight and they could find lodgings. Hildegard missed her family and was concerned for them. It was bad enough that her father had been in hospital for the past 10 years. The women had become a team and depended upon each other. Hildegard considered she was the strong one and Mama and Gretel were having to cope without her. She didn't feel at all strong at this moment though as, along with being physically weak after this horrendous journey, she felt only sadness and anxiety as she considered the destruction and the loss and the uncertainty of their lives, their home and their country. As she focussed on the senseless killing of the people of Dresden and the many refugees who had already arrived there, Jaginne seemed further away than ever. A lifetime away. But Hildegard decided to snap herself out of worry and sadness and to instead count her blessings and pray again for the safety of her family and friends.

As they filed back onto the train the travellers were told they were headed for Carlsbad (now known as Karlovy Vary). In 1938 Hitler had invaded Czechoslovakia and annexed much of its western territories which included Carlsbad. The country was currently occupied by the German Army and was therefore a relatively safe destination for the evacuees.

Chapter 24

Carlsbad

One hour later on 16th February 1945, the train finally pulled into Lower Carlsbad Station. Slowly all the weak and exhausted travellers who were able, finally climbed down from the cold, dark and uncomfortable train for the last time and Hildegard retrieved her bicycle from the cargo truck. The station staff were helping the sick. Evacuees were divided into groups and each group was escorted to either a camp or other accommodation. Hildegard found herself split from Elisabeth who was taken to a camp with others. Hildegard was led, with other railway employees, to a disused school house just outside of the town. They were shown to a huge, dark and dingy room full of bunk beds; a makeshift dormitory. It was filthy. The refugees learned later that this temporary hostel had been previously used to house Italian prisoners of war and it was clear that little if any cleaning had been carried out since their departure. After food was provided and each refugee was de-loused, they all received a health check and were issued with all the necessary information they might need, including the fact that they would be notified as soon as jobs were allocated to them.

Trying hard to be pragmatic but failing miserably, Hildegard found herself a bed and, with the addition of a rough blanket, she tried to make herself as comfortable as possible. She forced some positive thinking, being glad that the bed was a lot more comfortable than the hard wooden benches or floor of the train on which she had tried to sleep for the past few nights. She was glad that at least the journey was over and they had finally arrived at this destination.

During the night, whilst trying to appreciate the bed and the safe environment, Hildegard, unable to sleep, noticed large beetles crawling over the walls and ceilings of the dormitory. This really was a disgusting place. Occasionally one of these enormous insects would fall off the ceiling and land on one of the beds. The next morning Hildegard saw that most of her colleagues' faces were covered in red spots, having been bitten by the beetles. For some reason she had not been bitten and she came to the conclusion that, thankfully, they didn't like her blood!

As early as possible the next morning Hildegard, glad the night was over, arose and, grabbing her belongings, left the hostel as fast as she could. Promising herself that she would not be spending another night in that dreadful insect ridden place, she found her way quickly into town to the camp where her fellow refugees were staying whilst awaiting news of jobs and accommodation. She was hoping to find her mother and sister at the camp but none of the railway employees, all having travelled without their families, had any idea where their family members had been taken.

There were many camps housing refugees in Carlsbad and Hildegard searched them all in the hope of finding her family. Unfortunately, though she found some of her fellow villagers, her mother and Gretel were nowhere to be seen. After such a comprehensive search she realised she had to settle for the fact they had been taken to another town, but which one was a mystery.

Hildegard had made the decision that on no account would she return to the filthy hostel and instead, for now, she would stay at the camp. It was better, but not much better. It was also cold and uncomfortable and there was very little food, but she had friends there and her cousin Elisabeth and she found comfort in those familiar faces.

Many of the locals in Carlsbad were decidedly anti-German due to the commandeering of their country by Adolf Hitler and the subsequent German occupation, and therefore felt no trust or warmth towards these uninvited guests. The residents of Carlsbad were a mix of those who felt sorry for the expellees who had suddenly arrived en-masse in their town through no fault of their own, and those who were not so soft hearted and referred to them as 'those bloody refugees', who saw the weary and reluctant travellers as nothing more than a nuisance.

A few days after moving into the camp Hildegard decided to take a walk around the town to try and find herself somewhere better to stay. She hoped there might be a sign in a window. Having found no such sign, but not giving up, she noticed a lady walking towards her and, unsure of how she would be received, decided to take a chance and approach her. She asked her if she knew of anyone who had a room where she could stay for a few days. To her great surprise the lady seemed friendly and introduced herself as Anja. Although she said she didn't know of anyone, Hildegard went on to explain that she was staying in a cold and depressing camp with hundreds of other refugees and was desperate to find other lodgings. Anja, clearly moved by her story, said that her husband was in the Army and therefore away and then, astonishingly, asked Hildegard if she would like to stay in her spare room. She went on to tell her that she lived in a flat with her two children… a boy, Kurt, and a girl, Louisa. Hildegard could not have been more surprised and jumped at the chance. She was so fortunate to have met this dear lady who was literally inviting her to stay in her family home.

Without further ado, she went back to the camp, and to her fellow refugees' surprise, packed her bag and said her goodbyes. Anja took her to her modest and, as Hildegard immediately noticed, incredibly clean flat which appeared like a palace to her, and was led into the spare room with its comfortable bed and fresh linen. After the cold, cramped and uncomfortable conditions of the train, the disgusting hostel and little better camp accommodation, Hildegard thought she must be dreaming. Such an incredible blessing. She was so grateful to Anja and for the wonderful comforts of her new, if temporary, home.

After unpacking her few belongings Hildegard was happy to be able to properly wash for the first time since leaving home. She scrubbed herself clean and changed into fresh clothes. She felt like a new person. To prove she was a grateful house guest, Hildegard helped Anja with the chores, assisted with the cooking and looked after the two children if their mother needed to go out. Hildegard could still barely believe she had the benefit of a room to herself with a comfortable bed and food, and felt rather guilty that most of her colleagues and friends and neighbours had to make the best of the camp.

However, despite her newfound home, the reality of war was never far from Hildegard's thoughts. It was February 1945 and, so far during this long war, she had never been concerned about air raids, until now. Carlsbad itself had not suffered any bombing itself or nearby during the war until November 1944, just a few months previously, when 4 bombs were dropped on a power plant north of Prague which was a mere 130km away. Of even more concern were the bombs recently dropped on Prague itself on 14th February, St Valentine's Day. On the latter occasion the American Airforce, due to bad weather affecting their radar, were mistakenly of the opinion they were bombing Dresden! However, the fact that Czechoslovakia had been relatively safe thus far and that the Prague bombing was a mistake, in this time of war it became clear there were no guarantees.

One night Hildegard had left some washing drying outside and ventured out to collect it. A neighbour saw her and said "Get inside. Leave your washing!" Experiencing the nervousness and fear of locals, Hildegard would then lie in her bed praying that no bombs would drop. Every night Anja would take her children down a nearby mine, a make shift air raid shelter, to return home the next morning covered from head to toe in black soot. Anja would say "You should come down the mine with us and be safe". Hildegard would lay her fears to one side and reply "I would rather die than go down that black mine". The mine itself was a dangerous place. People had to take a lift down the mine shaft and at the bottom they would wade through water to find somewhere dry and try to get comfortable for the night. Hildegard, taking everything into consideration, decided "No, I would rather take a chance and stay in my bed."

Just two weeks after moving into Anja's home, Hildegard was informed there was a job for her at the one of the railway stations in Carlsbad and, in addition, she had been assigned permanent accommodation. She had been very happy with Anja and her children and was very sad to leave them but leave she must and, after fond farewells and many thanks, she once again packed her bag and made her way to the house of the Station Inspector, Klaus

Hoffmann, where she was again given a room of her own. The staff of the local railway stations were compelled to give a room to a refugee who had been given a job on the railway. Hildegard was grateful she was not made to feel a nuisance with this arrangement as the Inspector was a kind man, and she really liked his wife Bernice and their daughter Brigitta.

The next day Hildegard left her new lodgings to start her new job in the office at *Unter* (Lower) Carlsbad Railway Station. She soon settled into the job and familiarised herself with the running of the office. Many of her old colleagues were also given jobs there so she felt quickly at home. Some friends were not so fortunate and were unable to obtain a job or lodgings and they were forced to remain in the camp. Hildegard was very grateful to have a comfortable place to stay, with a very nice family and also have the opportunity to earn money again so that she could buy the things she needed. Money and food were not plentiful for anyone and it was a stretch for households to feed the refugees they were bound to accommodate. A young local man Hildegard worked with at the station was the son of a local butcher and she was occasionally fortunate to receive a bag of sausages or other meat from him to take home to Frau Hoffmann.

The future was uncertain and she had no idea of the whereabouts of her mother and sister but Hildegard was glad to be out of possible danger at the hands of the Red Army and was beginning to feel more settled, safe and secure.

Although glad of the opportunity to earn money, the devalued Deutsche Mark caused Hildegard to live frugally in order to be able to save for her return fare to Jaginne, whenever that might be. The war raged on but, with Hitler still hiding in his bunker, Hildegard and her colleagues were beginning to feel hopeful that the fighting would soon finally to come to an end. In the meantime though, the war continued and the threat of being bombed was always there.

25th of March was Palm Sunday and Hildegard and her friends had attended an early service at church and were back at the camp drinking coffee and chatting. There had been no air raids since the sudden and misdirected raid on Prague on 14th February, just two days before their arrival in Carlsbad. Suddenly and to Hildegard's horror, just before noon sirens sounded and it was necessary to retreat immediately to the nearest bomb shelter. This was her first experience of an air raid and also an air raid shelter and she wasn't impressed with the shelter. It was stuffy and cramped and now full of people, sitting and waiting. Eventually she heard the frightening sound of bombs dropping, apparently in the distance. The noise of aircraft and bombs exploding went on and on. Although a little reassured by her friends that the bombs were not falling in that vicinity she was still scared as the noise was deafening. Then, suddenly, all was quiet and eventually it was safe to venture outside. Hildegard still shaken after the experience and the volume of noise, was stunned to find her surroundings to be intact and unaffected. The raid, it was later revealed, had taken place 130kms away in Prague and it had been the first planned attack on that city.

Hildegard aged one year

The family home in Jaginne (now Jagienna)

Hildegard and Gretel

Hildegard 1937

Sisters in the snow

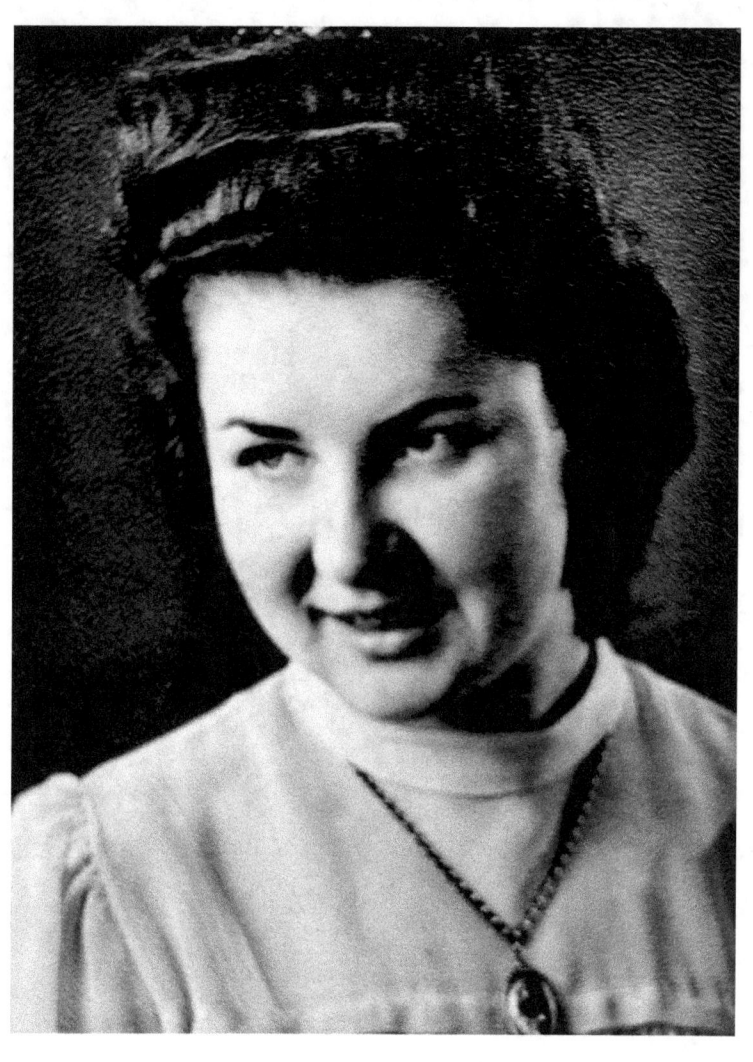

Pflichtjahr Convent girl 1940

Karl, the young recruit

The hotel bar in Glienick 1948

Hildegard's ID card February 1949

Gretel and Mama in Jagienna 1950

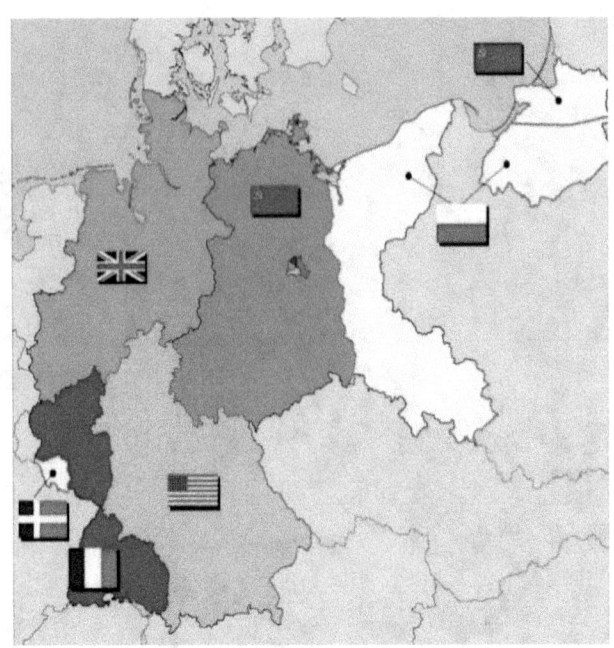

Map of Germany, February 1945, showing occupation zones, with the eastern territories being granted to Poland.

Karl and Hildegard on their wedding day in England 1951

Part Seven

1945 Post War Changes

Chapter 25

Czechoslovakia, a Dangerous Place

Carlsbad, situated in West Czechoslovakia, was historically a beautiful spa town, not unlike Bad Carlsruhe only much larger. Early 20th Century Carlsbad was situated in the Sudetenland region of East Germany, and therefore mostly German speaking, but was taken to become part of Czechoslovakia at the end of the Great War. From then, Carlsbad again became a thriving tourist centre for people coming from miles around to enjoy the spa waters.

Twenty years later, in 1938, Adolf Hitler reclaimed Sudetenland which included western Czechoslovakia as it was rich in natural resources and a successful centre of industry, not least due to the Skoda armaments factory. Czechoslovaks in general were becoming more and more tired of living under Hitler's occupation and regime and suffering under strict Nazi rule. Their main business as a spa town was significantly depleted and, with the loss of the main source of employment and income, residents found themselves struggling financially as money and food supplies were short and this added to the already rising tensions.

Two railway stations served the town. Situated 2km north of the *Unter* (Lower) Station where Hildegard was employed, was the sister station known as *Hohe* (Higher) Carlsbad Station.

It was two months since the refugees' arrival in Carlsbad and Hildegard, unaware of the unrest amongst townspeople and despite the threat of possible air attacks, was feeling a little more settled. There had been no bomb threats since Palm Sunday and she enjoyed the responsibilities of her work in the Unter Station office and was glad to be earning money again.

Occasionally Hildegard would be required to cycle to Hohe Station on an errand of some kind. After completing one such errand on 19th April, whilst cycling back to the Lower Station, air raid sirens began noisily telling people to find a shelter. Thankfully Hildegard spotted a nearby bunker, quickly left her bicycle and dived inside with others who'd been heading in the same direction. The bunker was essentially a large door in the side of a hill. Once inside she found a seat. Hildegard was not happy with this choice of air raid shelter and shivered with fear as she considered that, if a bomb fell nearby, the entrance could be blocked and they would be trapped and would all die.

All in the bunker were quiet. Waiting.

Soon came the droning sound of aircraft overhead, followed by a noise like all hell had broken loose. The sound was deafening. Much louder than her previous bunker experience. The noise of bombs dropping and the violent vibrations felt underfoot caused Hildegard to curl up in self-protection. With her head on her knees and arms wrapped over her ears and head, she prayed to God for safety. The noise continued. When would it stop? After a few seemingly never-ending minutes, suddenly, there was silence. No sirens. No aircraft. No bombs. Stillness. Except for straightening themselves up, no one moved. Each wondering what they would find outside. Each person feeling they were glued to their seat, reluctant to be the first to exit the bunker, dreading what they might see.

Finally, a brave man nodded to the rest and slowly and carefully opened the bunker door. He stepped outside, with others cautiously and nervously following.

As Hildegard emerged from the bunker she was confused by the sight. She'd expected devastation but everything around her was intact. Despite the level of noise and vibrations they had experienced in the bunker, there was absolutely no damage. Hildegard and others emerging from the bunker breathed sighs of relief as they realised that, despite the volume, the bombs must have been dropped elsewhere, hopefully far away. Still shaken, she found her bicycle and decided to return to her lodgings as it was by now the end of her working day. She was relieved to see the Inspector's house still standing. The moment she entered the house Bernice came rushing towards her in a fearful state. "I'm worried about my Klaus and Brigitta!" she cried. "They have not come home yet. I'm worried they've been injured or killed by the bombs!"

Hildegard immediately jumped back onto her bicycle and sped along the road to the Unter Station. On arrival she could not believe her eyes. She could not take it in. Terror gripped her very being. As if in slow motion she got off her bicycle and let it fall to the ground. An eerie stillness and silence filled the air. Nothing could have prepared her for the sight before her. She was aware of the terrible wreckage all around but much much worse than that were the bodies. Everywhere she looked there were dead bodies, and bits of bodies. Everywhere. Even hanging from trees. Bodies strewn all over the station. Hundreds of people had been killed that day whilst bombers destroyed the railway station and track.

"Go back! Go back!" She was suddenly aware of voices shouting at her which shook life back into her body. She shouted back "But I left my bicycle!" "OK get it quickly and GO!" She grabbed her bicycle and sped towards her lodgings, the realisation dawning on her that she didn't know which friends and colleagues were alive or dead. The railway station and the surrounding area had been bombed hard. If she hadn't been sent on the errand she would have been among the dead.

Hildegard arrived back at the Inspector's house in a daze. Bernice was at the door asking her urgently "Did you see anyone alive?" Hildegard told her what she saw and said "I'm so sorry. I don't know if Klaus or Brigitta are alive" quickly adding "I'm sorry but I have to leave now. I've got to go to the camp!" She needed to go and see who amongst her friends were still alive. She quickly threw her belongings into her suitcase, grabbed her bicycle and, with her luggage balanced on the handlebars, set off as fast as she could towards the camp thinking "Carlsbad is a dangerous place and I've got to get out of here." She was in shock and desperate to go home whilst wondering would her life ever be normal again.

When struggling to push her heavily laden bicycle laden along the road leading to the camp, she saw an obviously distressed mother with her child. As Hildegard approached her, the young woman asked "Where are you going?" "I'm going to the camp where my friends are staying," replied Hildegard. "Can I come with you?" asked the woman. "My camp is deserted and I don't know where my friends have gone." Hildegard agreed and they walked the mile or so to the camp together. On arrival Hildegard exclaimed "Oh no. Everyone has gone! What do we do now?" This camp was also deserted so they decided to walk back towards the town. There were lots of people around, mostly dashing towards the station to give help or desperately looking for loved ones but they saw no one they knew. They were cold and it was late and darkness was falling. With no clue as to what to do next, the young women and the tired, weeping child sat on a bench anxiously considering where they might sleep until morning when they would resume their search. An elderly man passing by heard the child's sobs and asked if there was anything he could do to help. After explaining their predicaments, the man offered them a room in his flat for the night. They were tired, hungry and thirsty so, deciding to take a risk with this stranger due to there being no other option, they thanked him and followed him. The man's kindness more than made up for the flat's lack of cleanliness. The three were so grateful to him for sharing what little food and drink he had, together with providing them with a safe place to sleep for the night.

The next day, after thanking the man for coming to their aid and for his generosity, the young women decided to part and go their separate ways in search of people they knew. They were both grateful for each other's company and wished each other well.

Hildegard headed back to the camp hoping her friends would do the same. It was with huge relief later that morning when some colleagues from her station returned explaining that they'd been moved to a different camp overnight for their safety. They had been saved from the bombing due to the rota putting them on different shifts. All were happy to be alive but devastated for the friends who weren't so fortunate.

Chapter 26

Decisions

Later in the day Hildegard found more bewildered evacuees drifting back to the camp. No one felt safe now. She was considering what to do next when she spotted her cousin Elisabeth. They immediately ran to each other with hugs and tears of relief that the other was alive. Hildegard said, "I want to go back home. Will you come with me?" Elisabeth didn't answer so Hildegard urged her, "The Russians will have left Jaginne by now and it will be safe. Please say you'll come with me!" Elisabeth didn't want to upset her cousin but had to say "I'm so sorry Hilde. I'm not going back. I'm waiting for Mitchgy and will stay with him." Mitchgy was a man who Elisabeth had been seeing for a while. This was a great blow to Hildegard as she did not relish the thought of trying to find her way home on her own.

Wrestling with disappointment, she realised that walking back home alone would be far too dangerous. Neighbouring Breslau was under siege and there was the continued threat of Russian soldiers. She felt sure she would get home at some point but for now she realised she had no choice but to stay at the camp with her friends until an opportunity to leave arose. At least she was with people she knew.

April 1945 and Adolf Hitler was reunited with his girlfriend Eva Braun in his bunker and they married. Then suddenly, on the 30th of that month, came news that the Fuhrer was dead. Details were divulged that he had shot himself in his bunker after he and his new wife had taken cyanide capsules. People were now able to talk openly of his many and most heinous crimes and that due to his greed and mad ideologies, he had started this dreadful war with millions of both Military and civilians dead and towns and cities brought to the ground. The next piece of news came on 2nd May that East Berlin had succumbed to Russian occupation. Surely now the war will come to an end.

By this time most areas of Germany were beginning to experience French, British, American or Russian Military occupation. The one remaining area still holding out for victory was the Fortress town of Breslau. Hitler's orders had been very clear and even though he was dead those orders to defend the town, whatever the cost, still remained. However, with a death toll already amounting to tens of thousands, on 6th May, Garrison Commander General Hermann Niehoff made the decision to surrender to the Red Army. The Siege of Breslau marked the end of one of the most savage battles in modern history and accounted for one of the largest number of deaths in battle during WWII.

Two days later on 8th May the war was declared to be over and the Allies celebrated Victory in Europe.

On hearing this much longed for news the sense of relief at the camp was palpable. The war was finally over. Some were incredulous, barely allowing themselves to believe this new and sudden information. Many were elated and dancing with joy. The initial consolation was short lived for most in the camp however, as the refugees began to consider what to do next. They were all far from home, not knowing what had happened to their dwellings and many with no idea of the whereabouts of loved ones. Their newly found freedom was not straightforward. Suddenly countless displaced and essentially homeless expellees found themselves in the unenviable situation of having to make big and difficult decisions about what to do and where to go now the war had ended.

Meanwhile in Carlsbad, and in Czechoslovakia as a whole, there were stirrings. The country which had been under Nazi rule for the entirety of the war was no longer a safe place for Germans.

Hildegard was even more desperate to leave Carlsbad. On hearing that changes were happening which could render her and her fellow countrymen in danger, she was even more determined to leave. For her the decision whether or not to return home was an easy one. There was nowhere else she would rather be and she would take her chances regarding the risks involved. She couldn't rest so she continued to search for friends and neighbours from Jaginne who'd be willing to make the journey home with her. Disappointingly each person she found who lived anywhere close to her village said no. All were concerned and fearful of what they might find and of the Russian occupation and all that might mean. Most stated they would rather stay in the hope that the English or American Military would come and help them. Hildegard was surprised and upset that no one wanted to return home. She realised that the journey could be a difficult and maybe treacherous one and due to the destruction of the railway, and doubts that any alternative transport would be available, she would be forced to travel on foot.

After the Carlsbad bombings the 1st Czechoslovakian National Revolutionary Council, with the assistance of the American Military, took over the administration of Carlsbad from German troops. On 11th May the Red Army arrived and announced that all ethnic Germans resident in Czechoslovakia were having their properties confiscated and were to be evacuated west into Germany. All the eastern territories were now officially under Russian occupation.

Now every ethnic German was being given no choice but to leave Czechoslovakia immediately and move west into Germany. Expelled again. German refugees and German townspeople alike, were all panicking and packing and on the move. Hildegard, carrying her belongings, moved amongst hundreds of displaced people still hoping to find someone to join her on the eastward and more dangerous journey home but no one was brave enough to go with her into the now Russian-occupied east. They felt there was no going back but instead resigned themselves to go where the authorities wanted them – on German soil. Just as she was ready to give up the search, join the majority and unwillingly go with them, she bumped into the boss of her old station at Carlsruhe. Franz Hellmann was with his sister Agatha and her daughter Marta. They had not come across each other at all during their time in Carlsbad but they told Hildegard they also wanted to go home and would be glad if she'd join them on the journey! This was excellent news.

Hildegard was elated and relieved to have found travelling companions and the group made plans for their immediate departure. Franz remembered he had seen an old discarded wagon so he set off to find it to convert it into a hand cart for their luggage. The four friends prepared themselves for the long journey home. There was no choice but to walk. Over 400km (250 miles) of autobahn stretched out before them but there was no alternative.

On that spring day, with their luggage piled into the hand cart, the group bravely set off on the longest walk of their lives, aware of possible dangers ahead yet determined to return to the place they called home.

All signposts had been destroyed so the autobahn was the best route to take with the long straight roads making it easier to travel in the right direction and stay on track. On reaching the autobahn they were surprised to see so much activity. As well as many Military vehicles such as tanks and trucks travelling in both directions, hundreds of refugees had the same idea of using the autobahn to begin their journeys either east or west. Those travelling east, like Hildegard and her group, were mostly trying to get back home but others just wanted to get out of the Russian zone by travelling south-west to the American zone or north west to the English zone. Either of the latter zones were preferable to that controlled by the ruthless and hate filled Russians.

Chapter 27

Another Journey Begins

As she walked Hildegard thought of home. What will she find there? Was her house still standing? There was even a tiny hope in her heart that her mother and sister might be there? She doubted it but whether or not they were alive was the much more important question constantly on her mind. These concerns and the desire to be home drove her forward.

The throng of refugees they had initially encountered had dispersed. Most it seemed were travelling west in the opposite direction and to safety whilst Hildegard and her group were more or less alone now and staying alert to possible dangers ahead in the Russian zone. Sometimes Franz on hearing the rumble of tanks or armoured vehicles in the distance would say "Quick! Under cover!" This was a regular occurrence and the group would quickly move behind a building or trees or whatever cover was available and lay low until any vehicle passed.

Hildegard, Agatha and Marta rubbed soil into their faces and their clothes were ragged enough to pass for harmless old peasants so that, if they were seen by Russian Military, they wouldn't be of any interest to them. But nevertheless, they aimed to keep out of sight just in case. Franz and Agatha were determined to keep the younger women safe so were constantly vigilant.

These were dangerous times for Germans in the east. Instead of improving the lives of the German population as Hitler had proclaimed, he had destroyed the country. Millions were dead and now millions displaced. Hitler had made enemies of all of Europe and surrounding countries. None more so than Soviet Russia. Every German life was in danger of retaliation, especially if found in the wrong place. Such was the hatred and distrust that Russian soldiers did not hold back in their desire for retribution.

They were extremely dangerous. Men would be shot or hauled off to concentration or work camps for simply being German, and no German woman was safe. Thousands had been mutilated and killed during the months of the evacuations.

As night began to fall, the group began looking for somewhere to sleep for the night. Franz spotted a farmhouse which looked to be possibly unoccupied due to a lack of light shining from within. He knocked at the door and as there was no answer, he cautiously went inside. After a short while he beckoned to his fellow travellers that it was safe for them to enter. In the darkness they could see the house looked untidy and strangely there was a full pot of soup on the stove. Hildegard was hungry and set about trying to heat it up. "No!" exclaimed Klaus. "Don't touch the soup! It could be poisoned!" On further inspection they thankfully found some bread and other morsels to eat which were considered to be a safter option. As they gratefully ate and talked, they came to the conclusion that this house belonged to people who had needed to leave in a hurry so had grabbed what they could and fled. That night, after walking for most of the day and evening, the little group was very grateful for this roof over their heads and a place to rest and sleep.

The next morning began another day of walking. Each time they came upon a farm or a garden they would search for food. It seemed that every property had been deserted so they felt that any edible fruit or vegetable they were fortunate enough to find was theirs for the taking. At this time of year gooseberries and raspberries were in season but of course many had got there before them and stripped the fields and bushes of anything edible. In these days of war and worthless money, food was like gold dust. Even the Military would clear fields of their produce. Hildegard and her friends were happy to find anything at all that they could eat. Occasionally they would come across a couple of carrots or apples to share. The group more or less lived on carrots and apples throughout the entire journey.

They walked and walked throughout the day and overnight would hope to find an empty farmhouse or barn. Repeating the same routine where Franz would enter first to inspect the building and check what or who might be there, ensuring it was safe for the women to follow. There was always the possibility that there would be other refugees in a property but that was to be expected and they would try and make the best of it. Sometimes, but not often, there would be a little food to share. They were all in the same situation, weary refugees dragging their belongings for miles along the autobahn, trying to return to homes that may well now be occupied by strangers. It was an anxious time for them all. Some travellers were not doing so well and had become ill and could go no further. Hildegard counted her blessings that although exhausted and tired and hungry, she and her friends were fit and well enough to keep walking.

One night the group stayed in a barn next to a farmhouse. Franz went inside to check it out and a dozen or so people were already there. He beckoned to Hildegard, Agatha and Marta to enter and they nodded polite greetings to the other refugees. It was wise not to speak as no-one knew who they could trust. Best to keep your nationality unknown. The friends found a dark corner and made themselves as comfortable as they could on bales of hay hoping they could get some sleep.

Suddenly they heard loud voices coming from outside. The language spoken was Russian and Franz and Agatha quickly rearranged themselves so they were in front of the girls with their dusty faces. The women quickly made sure their headscarves were in place and hunched themselves over to look like frail elderly peasants, hoping they would fool whoever was about to enter. Hildegard prayed. The voices got louder and in burst four Russian soldiers. Each was armed with a rifle and two of them were shining torches in the refugees' faces. One roared "So, who wants to party?" The soldier had obviously been drinking a substantial amount of vodka. It became clear from the shouting and laughter of his colleagues that they had too. They were staggering under the influence of too much alcohol and flashing their torches erratically all around the barn. No-one moved or responded. "Ok," the soldier mumbled in annoyance, "There's nothing for us here. Let's go!" and the men drunkenly crashed about trying to get out of the door. The refugees kept still and quiet until the noise subsided and the soldiers went to find the next group of unsuspecting refugees. When all in the barn felt it was at last safe to breathe again, eyes met in mutual relief. "That was close", Hildegard whispered to Marta. As she lay down to sleep, she thanked God for keeping them all safe and saving them from a most terrible fate.

Chapter 28

Risks and Threats

Young German women were constantly at risk of being abducted by members of the Red Army. If girls weren't taken by force, it was common practice for them to 'invite' them to a party where there would be lots of food. As so many were starving this was very tempting and many in their innocence went with them, mostly never to be seen again.

The risk the refugees were taking was great but with each day they were a little nearer to home. Along the road they would occasionally see a dead horse, just left there by the side of the road. The hot sun was not helping. It seemed to be getting hotter each day and there was little shade along the autobahn. Hildegard's shoes were so worn that she barely had any sole left. The hot dusty ground burned her feet through the holes. Many didn't make it to their destination. As well as dead horses they would sometimes come across a dead person, often elderly, who had collapsed and was just left there, by the side of the road. Hildegard couldn't look. Even worse than that to her was the occasional person slumped and still alive but unable to walk another step, hoping someone would be able to help them. But none of the refugees could help as they were all struggling to stay upright themselves. As hard as it was, they had no choice but to keep walking and looking forward. Shocking and heartbreaking sights to see. It was so wrong.

Each day was the same, with the group using their eyes to scan their surroundings for danger and also in the hope of finding the occasional morsel of food. Then, as light began to fade, they would begin looking for somewhere to spend the night, often having to veer off the autobahn whilst all the time looking out for Russian soldiers. Franz and Agatha did their utmost to keep

Hildegard and Marta safe. Hildegard was so grateful to these kind people for taking care of her and protecting her from harm.

Another night, on the outskirts of a village, the group found a farmhouse in which to spend the night. Other refugees had got there first but there was room for Hildegard and her companions. There became an unspoken code amongst the refugees that they were all in this together and there was no room for selfishness.

After a much-needed night's sleep, early next morning the group awoke to the most amazing smell of freshly baked bread. Everyone was starving and desperate for food, not least Hildegard. Knowing it was a big risk, she suggested to Agatha that they go out and try and get some of the bread which was obviously being baked just a few metres away. Agatha reluctantly agreed and the two women carefully picked their way along the street until they could see the bakery. As there was no one to be seen, they quickly went inside the shop. The man behind the counter looked at them with a stony glare. Agatha quickly greeted him in Polish. Silence as the man stared at her. She continued, "We are starving", she said. "Can we please have some bread?" "No!" came the firm reply, also in Polish. "I could be shot. The bread is for Russian soldiers." Agatha began to explain to the man how they had been walking for days in an attempt to get home and how they had had been living on rotting fruit and vegetables, whatever they could find. He continued to stare blankly at her as she begged and pleaded with him. Agatha eventually realised that her efforts were a waste of time and gave up. The two took their leave and quickly made their way back to the farmhouse.

Agatha was so disappointed having to give her brother and daughter the bad news that they'd been unsuccessful, but as she began to apologise to Franz and Marta, a smiling Hildegard suddenly produced a large loaf of bread from inside her coat! And then another! Her friends could scarcely take it in. It was as though they had come across a pot of gold. The worth of this bread was immeasurable. The first filling food they'd had for days. There was plenty to go round and the bread was immediately torn and shared amongst all the refugees in the farmhouse and, as the friends ate, Hildegard explained that, as Agatha kept the attention of the baker with her pleading, she stealthily popped one, then two loaves inside her coat without being seen. The friends and their new companions laughed with happiness and gratitude as they savoured every mouthful of the wonderful and delicious bread.

Continuing on their journey, after coping for so many bumpy miles, their trusty cart which had carried their luggage for the best part of this extremely long trek and which they had all taken turns to pull, suddenly broke and was beyond repair. From this point on, so as not to be hindered by excess weight, each decided that one bag per person was all they could manage. After sorting and repacking only what they could carry, they left the remainder of their luggage by the side of the road. Maybe another traveller would be grateful for a change of clothes. With their remaining rucksacks on their backs the four continued on their way.

Chapter 29

How Much Further?

Each day brought the weary group closer to home and, by the time they were approaching Breslau, night was falling and Hildegard knew they were only a day or so away from Jaginne. They were all aware and saddened by thoughts of the devastation that was wrought and the thousands who had fallen in this Siege Town.

As they searched for somewhere to stay Franz noticed a house at the end of a long driveway a short distance off the autobahn. They tentatively approached and it appeared to be vacant so, as usual, Franz went ahead to investigate. After disappearing inside for a while he emerged and beckoned for the rest to follow. Once inside Hildegard noticed the house was richly furnished with beautiful drapes and nice furniture. It became obvious that here was another family who had to flee in a hurry and it seemed they had taken very little with them. Taking a look around this opulent home, Hildegard and Agatha found wardrobes full of clothes in beautiful bedrooms. And there were shoes! Hildegard was so desperately in need of a pair of comfortable shoes as her feet were burned and sore from the hot surface of the autobahn. There was so little leather on the soles of her current pair that they were barely worth wearing and now, at just the right time, she found a sturdy pair of shoes that fit and would help her make the final part of the journey less painful. She was sure the owner would understand. She then spotted another pair she really liked and, realising that if she didn't take them another refugee would, she slipped those into her rucksack as well. She was so grateful.

The next morning, the travellers continued along their way, every step taking them nearer towards home. Hildegard, whose legs and feet were sore from walking, felt grateful to be wearing strong and comfortable shoes for the first time in days. Finally, after ten gruelling and exhausting days, they safely reached

Carlsruhe, the home town of Franz, Agatha and Marta and it was time to say goodbye. There were hugs and tears. Hildegard expressed her gratitude to these dear friends for their company. She didn't know where she would be now without their help and company and encouragement. It was then that she realised she was now on her own for the first time and she felt anxious about what she might find in Jaginne. "I'm worried that there will be no one in the village when I arrive and I'll be there on my own!" she exclaimed. "You will be fine Hilde," said Franz. He quickly wrote on a scrap of paper which he handed to her saying "Here is my address. If you find you are alone then all you have to do is come to Carlsruhe and you can stay with us!" Hildegard thought, "Well I've come this far. Just 4km and I'll be home. And I'll decide what to do next when I get there." "Thank you so much" she said, hugging each of her friends again, "And thank you for taking care of me. You are good friends." She could never have coped with that journey alone and was so very grateful to them all and especially for Franz and Agatha's protection.

Chapter 30

Allied Occupation and Denazification

The summer of 1945 and the Allies were in full control of a defeated Germany and beginning the huge clean-up campaign. First was to ensure that atrocities like the holocaust would never happen again. Allied Forces continued to scour the country to find death camps, concentration camps and prisoner of war camps, releasing those who had been interned over the duration of the war and before. Conditions in most camps was found to be squalid and dehumanising. Prisoners comprised Jews, Poles, Slavs, Romas and Freemasons, suspected Communists, anyone not upholding Nazi ideology and also criminals. Out of the millions of prisoners there were over 13million deaths by execution, starvation, or generally poor conditions.

The second major part of the campaign was for the Allies to undertake the systematic denazification of the 70million brainwashed German people, the country's administration and judiciary and its culture. Indoctrination had been so intense that Naziism had taken over every single facet of the lives of the German people.

Over 8million members of the Nazi party made up around 10 percent of the population and the most committed were hunted down and intensively questioned, resulting in many arrests for crimes against humanity. Trials were carried out in Nuremburg, though the search for the most heinous Nazi murderers went on for years. The German people needed to know and believe that their leaders were no more than common criminals. The swastika was banned but breaking down the Nazi mentality was extremely hard. It would be a long time before the population would be able to greet each other without adding the automatic declaration of Heil Hitler together with the Nazi salute.

British, French and American troops, in their zones of occupation, helped supervise repair work in order to get Germany back on its feet. The British instigated Operation Coal Skuttle and released prisoners to work in the mines and reconstruct roads and railways so as to provide the population with the necessary coal and wood needed in their homes. So many bombed streets resulted in people living in depravation and reduced to sleeping in air raid shelters. New ration systems were set up. A new German Police Force was created with the understanding that this new Force was the servant of the people and not their master. So many beliefs to be undone and rebuilt in the German psyche. Teachers needed to be retrained to eradicate Naziism from the curriculum.

The defeated Germans were at a loss to know what to do as they had been so accustomed to following the Fuhrer's instructions in their everyday lives. Allied troops had to re-educate as well as repair. Another task for the Allies was to deal with the 50,000 a day requests for missing persons.

Added to all of this was the even bigger and more pressing burden of the Cold War effectively caused by Military tension between Germany and Russia. Russia was now the new main enemy. The Soviet Union had control over East Berlin with a Communist leadership causing the city to be divided.

Part Eight

1945 - 1946

Chapter 31

Almost There

Hildegard continued along the last leg of her journey home alone. Although the war in Europe was over, the Cold War continued and Russia's occupation of the eastern territories had completely changed the lives of all German people who had called East Germany and other East European countries their home. The Red Army continued to seek retribution. They were a force to be reckoned with and all Volksdeutsche, including Hildegard, realised they were to be avoided if possible.

The sun shone brightly over the fields but she had no energy to enjoy the familiar scene. She continued to keep close to the trees and hedges that were lining the dirt road, ready to find a place to hide should she hear any vehicles approaching. She could see all around that for now she was quite alone and she hoped and prayed it stayed that way. She was hungry and thirsty and beyond exhausted. So close to home but due to her weak and painful limbs she began to think she wouldn't make it. "Dear God please help me get home safely", she prayed.

The last kilometre was the hardest as each step seemed to make no difference at all. She was so tired and weak she feared she may collapse. Anxious thoughts tore at her mind. What will she find when she gets there? What would she do if faced with the Red Army? Though her strength and energy were depleted, there was no turning back. Then suddenly Hildegard spotted something glimmering across the fields in the distance. Could this be home in sight? The closer she got she realised it must be the cross on top of the spire of her village chapel.

Whilst painfully putting one foot in front of the other, she felt the chapel cross urging her forward telling her "You're almost there. Just keep going. You cannot give up now."

Finally, a dusty, dirty and bedraggled Hildegard arrived at her village. She could scarcely believe it. There was no sign of life and thankfully no sign of any Military. Instead, it was strangely quiet. As her sore legs took her slowly in the direction of her family home, she was comforted to see the forest and houses and fields of her beloved Jaginne spread out around her. There was a sound in the distance she couldn't determine. The sound became a little louder as she walked bravely on not knowing what it might be. Maybe the Red Army's presence, which caused her to tremble. She tried to focus on the sound as it seemed familiar – an everyday kind of sound. "It sounds like a lawn mower" she thought. Yes, she was sure it was a lawn mower. Surely Russian soldiers wouldn't be mowing the grass?

Chapter 32

At Home with the Jakubiks

Hildegard eventually saw a man, thankfully in civilian clothes, cutting the grass around a property near the edge of the forest and as she drew closer, she could see it was Peter Jakubik, her friend Else's father. He stopped mowing when he noticed the young woman approaching him. He looked at her blankly at first. He didn't recognise her. On the verge of collapse, she managed to say weakly "Peter! It's me. Hildegard." "I didn't recognise you Hildegard," said Peter. "You are so thin. Else is home. Let's get you in the house. Quickly. Come inside." Peter helped Hildegard into the house where Else was preparing food in the kitchen. "Hilde!" she exclaimed, and hugged her friend. "Come. Let me help you", as she took her bag and helped take off her coat. As Else took care of the weak and worn traveller, Peter continued with the food preparation as he could see she was half starved and desperate for nourishment. He prepared some scrambled eggs and bread. Else made her comfortable at the table and Hildegard ate. Other than the bread they had stolen in Breslau some days ago, this was the first good food she'd had in days.

After eating, Else said "Come now Hilde, you look so tired. Let me help you into bed and we'll talk tomorrow". Else helped her friend wash, and after providing her with a nightgown she guided her onto the bed, pulling the cosy *federbett* over her. Hildegard fell asleep immediately. She slept and slept. She slept for the rest of that day and night and all of the following day. When she finally awoke on the evening of the second day, she couldn't remember where she was. She had been dreaming and that, together with the nightmare of the past weeks, had left her in a very confused state. She finally remembered Peter and Else and relief flooded over her with the realisation that she was safely home again, with food and a bed and dear friends who wanted to take care of her. Unimaginable relief.

Else, who had been regularly checking on Hildegard, concerned as to the length of time she had been asleep, came into the room, relieved to see she was finally awake. "I'll get you something to eat" she said whilst disappearing out of the door. She quickly came back with food and drink knowing that her friend would have a lot of questions to ask, especially about the whereabouts of her mother and sister. As she sat on the edge of the bed helping Hildegard with the food, Else said "I'm so glad I am back in Jaginne so that I can take care of you."

Else explained that her father, despite being an ethnic German had been told to stay in the village as he and his blacksmith business were of vital importance to keep the hooves of Russian soldiers' horses healthy and reshoed. He had no choice. His wife, his two sons and two daughters were forced to evacuate without him. Else had been anxious regarding her father's wellbeing and had found transport to return home. She was also hoping to be reunited with her boyfriend. During the war Else had worked in the local village shop and was in love with the young Polish owner, Siegmunt Charm. On her return Else had found that his business had been confiscated by the Russians and he had been arrested for speaking out against Communism. He had been sent to a prison camp to work on the bridge in Gdansk. She hoped and prayed that one day he would be released and they would be together again.

"I'm sorry to say I have no news of your mother and Gretel", said Else. "I am also concerned about my own mother and the rest of my family as they will have been moved to another camp by now but I have no idea where or how they are." The two girls looked at each other with great sadness as they thought about their loved ones, not knowing whether they were alive or dead.

"The Russians come here regularly," continued Else, "so we must be very careful and stay hidden. We all know what the Russians have been doing to women and we know what they would do to us if they had the chance so we must stay alert and keep completely out of sight if we hear them coming. Russian soldiers are brutes.

"The good news is that your house is still standing. We will go there when you feel stronger and see how it is."

After a few days of rest and good food, together with the kindness and care given by Else, Hildegard's health and strength showed signs of improvement. Else asked her "Do you have the energy to take a little walk to your house?" Hildegard thought she did and the two girls set off down the lane. It was a mere few months since the expulsions yet her lovely home looked unkempt with the gardens and fields overgrown. As they approached, they immediately noticed that the front entrance door, which her mother had carefully bolted as they left, was hanging off its hinges and was peppered with bullet holes. Walking inside they saw devastation. Their few pieces of furniture had been knocked over and much was smashed and broken, obviously thrown about as the Russian soldiers searched the property for items of value. Still hanging on the wall was a framed picture of Karl, the young man Hildegard had been writing to, dressed in his Army uniform. It shocked her to see that a bullet had been shot through the middle of it. Hildegard was numb as she looked around the house but suddenly felt a surge of gratitude that she, her mother and sister had fled in time. She was glad that her father was safe in the hospital and had not had to face evacuation and then to return to this. Dear Papa, she hadn't been able to visit him for months now.

As they left the house Hildegard looked over to the meadow and a brief moment of positivity swept over her as she noticed the familiar sight of the clusters of fresh white margueritas, taking her back to happier days. As the flowers stood straight and tall in the bright sunshine, they spoke a message of survival and hope in the midst of ruin and dereliction.

Always listening and watching for approaching horses or vehicles, Else suggested taking the longer route back to the forge so that Hildegard could see more of the village. As they walked Hildegard was aware of the absence of life, but something else was different. Her eyes surveyed the area and as she looked beyond the meadow she saw three graves. She'd have passed by them on the day she arrived home but hadn't notice them. They were new. As the girls walked on there was another and then another. Graves of villagers. And graves of local soldiers killed in action. Else saw Hildegard's distress but was loathe to explain at this moment. "Let's talk about it later" she said.

Chapter 33

Painful Truths and the Kindness of Friends

Peter, busy in his forge, looked up when he heard his daughter and Hildegard approaching. He was relieved no Russians or Poles had apprehended them. Else said to her father "I think we should talk to Hildegard as she needs to know what happened after the evacuation".

Peter laid his work to one side, Else brought coffee, and as the three made themselves comfortable at the kitchen table, Peter very reluctantly explained that just a few hours after Hildegard and her family had left on that cold winter's night, the Red Army arrived in the village. Hildegard braced herself for what she was going to hear. Peter continued "They went from house to house searching for anything worth looting. As well as items of value, they were also looking for any remaining ethnic Germans.

"During that first day they found a rifle in the house of Gerhard Smolarzik who had decided not to leave. They used it to shoot him in the legs. He is now crippled and will never walk again. Animals!" Hildegard was shocked to her core.

Peter had no choice but to tentatively inform Hildegard of some very sad family news. The house of her father's brother Franz, his wife Franziska and 4 of their 5 children who lived two villages away, had been burnt down by the Russians. They had all perished. This was her cousin Elisabeth's family. She'd lost touch with her after leaving Carlsbad. Did she know? Hildegard shut her eyes in shock and horror. She had always dearly loved Tante Franziska. And poor Elisabeth. Hildegard put her head in her hands. That dear innocent family. They must have been terrified. "Why did they choose that family?" she cried. "They weren't singled out Hildegard. They had just not been able to gather themselves and their belongings and their children quickly enough to leave. The Russians had clearly decided to kill anyone who remained" explained Peter and then, loath to relate more bad news yet realising he had no choice, braced himself again to say "They then gathered all the remaining Germans together, including young Johann from Dammern who'd stayed back to help his father with the farm, and they were lined up and shot." Hildegard's heart seemed to fall to the floor. To think she'd been upset about the condition of her family home. These cold-blooded murders were beyond anything she'd ever feared would befall her friends and loved ones in these sickeningly hateful days. She felt complete devastation.

After the evacuation the Red Army had shown no mercy to any German left in the village – except for Peter who was of use to them. This was too much to comprehend. So many lives and families had been harmed and destroyed since the start of this senseless war? What was the point of it all? The war had come to an end, yet even now the retribution, hatred and barbarism continued. In fact, for them, life was much worse than during the war years.

Hildegard glanced across the table at Peter and noticed how much older he looked, compared to just 6 months ago, before all these horrors began. Her friends told her of other stories as time went on. They talked of the bombing and total destruction of the Castle in Carlsruhe. But for Hildegard another story broke her heart. Peter had to give her the tragic news that the Convent had been bombed and all her beloved nuns had been killed.

Life in Jaginne would never be the same again. Although the Red Army's presence seemed to have depleted, except for occasional visits to Peter's forge with their horses, they were now at the mercy of the Polish Police. Similar to the Soviet mindset, since Hitler's invasion of Poland at the beginning of the war, Polish thinking was to quite naturally lay blame at the feet of the entire German people for the slaughter of thousands of Poles. They had seen newsreels of the huge rallies where the population cheered in worship of their Fuhrer. In their minds those cheering people were as much to blame as Hitler himself. Peter told Hildegard how after the expulsions, and the Red Army had done their worst, Partisan Poles came into the villages to pillage and even kill, if there happened to be anyone left to kill. Poles had been given legal carte blanche to claim any home once occupied by a German. It was a wonder that Peter was still the only resident left in Jaginne.

Peter Jakubic had been a blacksmith serving Jaginne and surrounding villages and towns for many years and he now counted his blessings that his trade had kept him alive. He was considered an important tradesman to the Russian soldiers, not only to reshoe their horses but also to fix any trucks or motor cars that were brought to him needing repairs.

Although he was pleased in many ways that Else was back home with him, he was constantly concerned that the Russians would see her so he was determined to stay vigilant in order to keep her safe. He knew too many stories of atrocities and now he had Hildegard to worry about as well. Peter was pleased for Else to have her friend as company, but the burden he now carried to keep both girls safe from harm was huge. Although his concerns were not for himself, he was at risk of arrest and being sent to a Siberian work camp or worse for harbouring ethnic Germans if the girls were found.

Russian soldiers or Polish Police could suddenly appear at any time, so they were constantly looking out for them. As soon as Peter heard a sound resembling anyone or anything approaching, he would start to whistle a tune and the girls would scramble up into the loft of the barn and stay up there until he told them the coast was clear. They could spend hours at a time in the loft, which they had made comfortable for themselves. To pass the time would sew or make up ghost stories!

The Russian soldiers paid Peter to keep their horses' hooves in good repair. However, as money during those days was more or less worthless, the bartering with goods became common practice. The soldiers would pay Peter with stolen blankets or fabric, even parachute fabric. Anything they could lay their hands on. Peter gladly took whatever they had in payment but he would also barter for horseshoes for his business as, without those, he'd be of no use to them.

Hildegard's time with the Jakubics enabled her to work towards regaining her health and strength until she was fully recovered. Quite soon she felt at least able to help with the chores and cooking meals. There was always plenty of food as there were many deserted farms with no farmers to reap the harvest.

As well as completing household chores, the girls kept themselves occupied by using the fabric Peter had been given by the Russian soldiers to make clothes for themselves. The grey blankets were perfect for making coats and jackets and skirts and with the parachute fabric they were able to make all the underwear they needed as well as blouses. All sewing equipment was kept in the loft so not even a reel of thread could be detected by visiting soldiers. As far as the Police and Military were concerned Peter lived alone and he definitely didn't look the type to stitch in his spare time!

Else sometimes helped her father in the forge and she also had animals to feed as Peter owned a cow, a pig and some geese. The evenings were a time to relax as the Polish Police were off duty and soldiers would rather be drinking vodka in the bars in nearby towns than wasting time in their sleepy village. To bring some cheer to the girls Peter would play tunes on his comb, whilst listening for any noise suggesting danger. Other times he would quietly strum his banjo and Else and Hildegard would sing old folk songs. Else had a beautiful singing voice. Hildegard was so grateful for these generous hearted friends for keeping her sane and safe in these dangerous and uncertain times.

Peter also used the evenings to teach Hildegard basic Polish. Peter and Else already spoke the language fluently. Peter had taught himself over the years as it was good for his business. With Jaginne being so close to the Polish border, many of his customers were Polish. Else also spoke the language due to her Polish boyfriend and time spent working with him in his shop. Peter felt it important to teach Hildegard as soon as possible so that she could pass as Polish if the need arose. He also taught her a few basic Russian words and phrases she could use if necessary.

Peter made several trips to Hildegard's family home to carry out repairs and make it safe again. He was a good and generous man.

Chapter 34

Christmas is Coming

Time pressed on through the summer and autumn and suddenly December had arrived and snow was falling thick and fast with Christmas approaching. Hildegard had put on weight and regained her health over the past few months and was feeling much stronger. Both girls had contacted the Red Cross to try to find their mothers and siblings but no one could give them any news of their whereabouts so they jointly came to the decision that after Christmas they would try and get back over the border and attempt to find them. It was a long shot but the decision was easily made as both had had enough of hiding in Peter's house. This was no life for two young women and they had to do something.

As Christmas drew near, Peter was given two live capercaillies (a capercaillie is a wood grouse, similar to and the same size as a turkey) by the Russian soldiers in payment for his services, one of which they would roast on Christmas Day. "Let's make a Christmas cake" said Else one day. "But we don't have all the ingredients," said Hildegard. "We have flour and eggs but no sugar." The girls sat down to think about how and where they could get sugar. "I know of a shop in a village along the road to Oppeln which sells just about everything," remembered Else. So they put their heads together and came up with a plan.

Even though fully aware of the danger and the fact that the shop Else had decided they should head for wasn't much short of 30km away, the girls decided to make the trip and, with no other option, it would have to be on foot. Very early the next morning they took a large rucksack into which they had, with some difficulty, crammed one of the live capercaillies, which would be used to barter in exchange for the sugar. Hildegard tightened the neck of the rucksack around the bird's neck so it couldn't escape but leaving its head poking out to allow it to breathe. At 5am Hildegard helped Else heave the heavy rucksack on her back and they set off to embark on this very long trek for the sole purpose of acquiring the much-needed sugar.

The bird seemed to get heavier with each few steps. Else had been carrying the load for about an hour when she cried "Hilde, it's your turn now. Please take this bird. It's pecking at my neck." Hildegard reluctantly took her turn.

The journey was long, hard and very uncomfortable and after over 5 hours of trying to keep out of sight whilst continually keeping their eyes and ears open for approaching Russian soldiers, they finally arrived and found the little shop. They walked in and Else asked the shopkeeper in Polish if they could exchange their large bird for some sugar. "I'm afraid not", said the man. "I have so many capercaillies I don't know what to do with them. I don't need another one!" "But we've come so far!" cried Else. "We've been walking for hours and the bird has been pecking our necks. We really need some sugar to make a Christmas cake". The girls were fighting back tears of disappointment. A simple bag of sugar meant so much to them and they were exhausted after their marathon walk to get there. The man felt bad when he realised how important this was to them. "OK", he said, taking pity. "Take this." And he handed them a 2-kilogram bag of sugar. "But take the bird away as well. I really don't need any more." They both squealed with delight at their bag of sugar and expressed to the man how much this meant to them and how grateful they were.

The girls were so happy their uncomfortable and gruelling trip had not been in vain. They realised it wasn't as much sugar as they had hoped for but it was better than nothing and it was more than enough for the Christmas cake. However, they now had to embark on the long walk home and realised as they set off that they had to again put up with being pecked all the way home. "Why not set it free," suggested Hildegard. Else thought for a bit and, feeling the soreness of her neck, she opened the rucksack to free the capercaillie and shooed it away, leaving the two young women to complete the long return journey with a much lighter load and no pecked necks!

Peter was very relieved to see the girls walk through the door as darkness had fallen hours before. If the friends had been spotted by the Red Army they could have been shot – all for the sake of a Christmas cake! Else and Hildegard didn't dare tell Peter that they had risked their lives for a mere 2 kilograms of sugar.

The next day Hildegard and Else happily made their cake.

As Christmas approached, the friends made efforts to subtly decorate the living room and as they did so they both found themselves looking back over the years and remembering the fun and excitement of Christmases past, both feeling pangs of sadness and uncertainty as they wondered whether or not their families were alive. As Hildegard so often did, she prayed.

Peter was aware that the presence of the Red Army in the area had lessened. He had not had any visits for the repair of horses' hooves for some time but didn't want to presume they had gone for good. Although the Polish Police didn't have the same bad reputation as Russian soldiers, he decided they should all remain vigilant. He decided to keep his thoughts to himself though, at least for a while.

A few days before Christmas Hildegard ventured outside to collect wood from the wood pile and, keeping out of sight as always, she noticed someone heading their way in the distance. A few refugees had been returning to Jaginne and neighbouring villages so she wasn't that surprised but for safety's sake she should stay under cover. Eventually she could see it was a young returning soldier in full uniform with a kitbag on his back. She didn't recognise him and he seemed lost. As he tramped through the snow by Peter's house, Hildegard felt it was safe for her to come out of hiding. "Hello" she said, "I don't recognise you. Where are you going? Can I help you?" He told her he lived in a village a few kilometres away and he was travelling home after serving in the war. He then asked, "Can you please tell me your name?" The question was completely unexpected but, after quickly evaluating the situation, she made the decision that the young man presented no threat and answered "Hildegard Scheitza." "So you are Hildegard Scheitza!" he immediately exclaimed, amazed that the very person he was looking for was standing right in front of him. He continued excitedly, "I have come here to your village as I have a message for you. I met your mother near a camp in Neumark Kr Zossen when looking for my own family. When we realised the proximity of our villages she asked if I could visit Jaginne to see if I would find you here and tell you your mother and sister are well and to give you this." The young man handed Hildegard a piece of notepaper with an address written on it in her mother's handwriting, continuing, "She told me how you had all left separately and that she was very worried about her elder daughter as you had no means of getting in touch with each other. She had no idea where you were and she didn't even know if you were still alive, but she hoped you had made it back home as you had discussed."

Mother and Gretel were alive and well! This was the most wonderful news. Hildegard could scarcely believe what she was hearing. She thanked him, telling him how grateful she was that he had taken the trouble to find her. He said it was a pleasure but he begged her not to tell a soul about this meeting and his passing of information across the border and reminded her that if he was found out by the wrong people he would be in trouble.

After promising the young soldier she'd be very careful who she talked to, she ran into the house and brought out a package of bread and ham and fruit to show her gratitude and help him on his way. She thanked him again and bade him farewell.

Hildegard gathered the logs and took them inside. Checking first with herself that she was safe to give Else the good news she spilled it out excitedly. Else was so happy for her but at the same time anxious that she had no idea of her own family's safety and whereabouts.

The plan to search for their families in the new year had taken a different turn as Hildegard now had news of her mother and sister. But the girls decided to travel together as they'd arranged and, once in the West, they may go their separate ways.

Just a few days after Hildegard received good news from the passing stranger, a neighbour who had left with the rest of the village at the time of the expulsions, returned to their village. He came to see Peter as he had news of his wife and children. He knew where they were! Peter and Else were elated. Hildegard came to the door on hearing their jubilation. This was the most excellent news for them all. All three now knew their loved ones were alive and safe and they had information of their whereabouts.

Peter, Else and Hildegard made Christmas as festive and as meaningful as they could but the girls' minds were singularly fixed on finding their families.

Chapter 35

Risking Lives Crossing the Border

As soon as Christmas was over the girls made plans to depart. They had worked out the route they needed to take, firstly they would head towards the camp where Else's family was staying as that was not too far over the border. It was almost 250km (154 miles) along the autobahn and Hildegard made it clear she was not going to attempt to walk! The girls realised that their biggest problem would be the borders themselves. Some were more heavily guarded than others. They had no idea what lay ahead and whether or not they would succeed but they would do all they could to reach their mothers and siblings.

Peter was not at all happy with their plan and begged them not to go. He was well aware of the terrible dangers and spelled out to the girls what might happen to them, hoping to put them off. Other than their long journey to buy the sugar, they had barely left the house over the past months. Finally, realising there was nothing he could say that would stop them, he had no choice but to go along with the idea.

At the crack of dawn on the morning of their departure Else and Hildegard packed their bags with their warmest clothes, grateful for the fabric supplied by the Russian soldiers. Snow lay thickly on the ground and temperatures were close to freezing. Warm coats and boots were at the ready. They had no map but the plan was to get to the autobahn and walk in a westerly direction until they could beg a ride. Peter gave them tobacco, a loaf of bread and some bacon to pay for the ride and also some Deutsche Marks, completely worthless in Poland but which might be of use once across the border. They hoisted their bulging rucksacks onto their backs, said their goodbyes to a very concerned Peter, and trudged through the snow down the lanes in the direction of the autobahn, carefully keeping under cover of hedges and trees wherever they could.

Hildegard could barely believe she was embarking on yet another dangerous journey but this had to be done. And another in freezing temperatures! But she had no choice. She had to go to find her mother and Gretel.

After an hour or so they reached the autobahn where, this being a much wider road, they felt quite conspicuous and vulnerable as they considered the dangers they could be walking into. They constantly sought out possible hiding places should an army vehicle appear in the distance. As usual Hildegard prayed t God's protection and asked that He would take them safely to their mothers, knowing that the journey ahead was unpredictable and risky to say the least. Thankfully all was quiet with very few vehicles using the autobahn. As they walked and talked the girls both heard the sound of an engine coming from behind. They quickly moved behind some bushes and peered through the branches to assess the type of vehicle. It was an old open truck and they could vaguely see a man at the wheel. They decided to risk showing themselves so came out into the open and, though petrified, waved their thumbs at the driver. The truck slowed down and stopped. The man looked elderly and they hoped harmless so, mustering every ounce of courage, Else asked him in Polish if he would be kind enough to take them over the border in exchange for a bag of tobacco. The man seemed reluctant at first but the promise of tobacco was enough to convince him to help the girls. He let down the back flap of his truck so they could climb aboard. The man was Russian. If he suspected they might be ethnic Germans he may not have risked it but Else's command of Polish was obviously convincing. Even so, taking people over borders, whatever their nationality, was strictly forbidden. There were some large bins at the rear of the truck. The girls understood as he said gruffly in Russian "Get in those", gesturing towards the bins. "You realise that if I'm caught, I will be shot? And so will you! So, stay in the bins and keep still!"

The girls each climbed into a bin and huddled down for the long and uncomfortable journey ahead of them. The thought of seeing their mothers again helped them put up with the discomfort.

It was a strange and very unnerving journey alone in that bin. Hildegard wondered how Else was coping. Life for both of the girls had been far from easy since the evacuations. Although hiding in Peter's loft for all those months was dangerous, it was not as perilous as this current situation. Both girls were risking their lives in order to find their families. Hildegard dwelt on the fact that due to the events of the past year she had become a little more worldly wise and had gained courage and fortitude. She had experienced some threatening situations to date and had survived.

Thankfully there weren't too many bumps in the road thanks to Hitler's plans to make Germany a better place with its beautifully built new roads, his autobahns. Part of the plan was to improve transportation of both goods and the population. Every family would own a car and get from place to place easily. But then he started a war and all personal transport vehicles were commandeered for the war effort! Since that time the autobahns had been used mainly for transporting Military Personnel, trucks and tanks.

Many kilometres and 3 - 4 hours later Hildegard's thoughts were interrupted as she felt the truck slow down. It eventually came to a halt and all was still. There were loud voices. Russian soldiers shouting instructions possibly at their driver. Fear gripped her into a stillness she didn't think she was capable of. Aware of her heart beating faster, she slowly curled herself into an even tighter ball. Time seemed to stand still. The big question on her mind was will they make it over the border or will the Russian soldiers insist on inspecting the truck's load? Hildegard silently prayed "Lord please keep us safe and get us through." "This is it" she thought.

Though she couldn't understand a word at the time, and translated by Else later, a voice gruffly asked "What are you shifting?" "Nothing", lied the elderly truck driver. "Move on then", came the unexpected reply. Hildegard suddenly felt the truck move on, further and further across the border, further and further away from the Russian soldiers. She could scarcely believe it and held her breath until she felt it safe to breathe out a big sigh of relief and relax. They were safe. "Thank you, God", she quietly prayed.

After 1 - 2km, when their driver felt they were far enough over the border and away from the checkpoint, he stopped the truck, walked around to the back and let down the flap. "You're safe now" he called to the girls. They knocked the lids off the bins, unfurled their stiff cold bodes, scrambled out with their bags and climbed down from the back of the truck, relieved to be able to stretch their legs after being in such a cramped position for the past few hours. They each hugged the man and thanked him so very much for the huge risk he took for them. "That's ok" he said. They gave him the tobacco and some of the fresh bread and bacon they had brought in their rucksacks which he gratefully accepted. "Safe journey," he said and went on his way.

Hildegard and Else hugged each other in disbelief! Thanks to the brave truck driver, they had made it safely over the Polish/German border and into Western Gorlitz. Gorlitz had been wholly part of Germany before the Potsdam Agreement and Germany's surrender but now, with the Oder-Niesse Line (following the Oder and Lusatian Neisse rivers) running straight down the middle of the town, Eastern Gorlitz was now Russian occupied and part of Poland, whilst Western Gorlitz was still part of Germany and occupied by Allied troops.

For the first time in months the friends suddenly experienced the freedom of walking around normally and not hiding from anyone or being in fear of arrest or harm. They quickly forgot their frightening ordeal crossing the border as they set off on foot knowing that Else's mother's camp wasn't too far away and they were able to ask for directions in German without fear!

On arrival at the camp the girls passed through a pair of tall gates and into the grounds of what was once a school. They were instantly recognised and excitedly greeted by many familiar faces from home. Hildegard exclaimed "The whole village is here!" At least all the women and children who had survived the exodus of a year earlier! Very quickly Else found her mother and her siblings. They hugged and cried. It had been months since they had been together and they were overjoyed to see each other alive and unharmed.

Hildegard was also thrilled to see everyone and the girls were brought food and drink after their journey. The camp lacked home comforts but at least the refugees had a roof over their heads and were safe. The neighbours all wanted news of home. There were so many questions. Who is still alive being the most important one. Then, which houses are still standing? Neighbours and friends were all trying to decide whether or not it was worth going back to their homes where danger still lurked, or should they stay and make a new life this side of the border. Most planned to wait until spring when the weather improved and make their decisions then.

The girls stayed the night at the camp and the next morning Else said, "Hilde, this is really hard for me to say but do you mind if I don't travel with you to find your family? Now that I've found my mother again I haven't the heart to leave her. Not yet anyway. I'm so sorry. I feel I must stay here until we decide what to do next." "Please don't worry" replied Hildegard. "I can see how happy to are to be with one another again and I wouldn't want you to take any more risks for me. Please don't worry. I will travel by train and I will be fine." The last thing Hildegard wanted to do was to take Else away from her family. She understood her friend completely and she was feeling surprisingly confident to face this next part of her journey, albeit alone. An ethnic German in Germany was not so worrying due to the diminished threat from Russian Military. However, there was the small problem of paying for a train ticket. She had just finished packing her bag when Else came up to her and, with a broad smile on her face, held out a handful of notes and coins which she had collected from among the neighbours. Hildegard was overwhelmed with their kindness. They had nothing but gave her what they had.

Part Nine

1946

Chapter 36

Finding Family

After saying goodbye to all her friends who called "Come back with your mother and sister when you find them!" Hildegard walked to the railway station. She paid for her ticket to Neumark Kr Zossen in Saxony, and was told she would need to change trains 5 times. Neumark was another 230km (150 miles) away so the journey would be a long one and not straightforward but, as she boarded the train, she felt happy and hopeful that by the end of the day she would be reunited with her mother and sister.

Many hours later, after an arduous journey, changing trains and locating connections, Hildegard finally arrived at her destination, cold, tired and hungry. It was almost 10pm as she stepped out of the station and onto the snow-covered streets. She had asked the Station Master for directions to the address the young soldier had given her. There was no one about and she felt scared and alone in this strange city. She was shivering with nerves and the cold and she prayed "Dear God, please help me find my mother." Just then she saw a man approaching. He was running along the road with his dog. He stopped when he saw Hildegard and asked if she needed help. She asked him if he knew The Fabrick which was the area she needed to find. He said he knew it and that he could show her the way.

The man was very kind and they talked as they walked and Hildegard told him she was searching for her mother and sister. She explained they had been separated at the time of the expulsions a year ago and they had completely lost contact with each knowing nothing of the others' whereabouts until recently. She told him her family had no idea she was looking for them.

Hildegard was grateful for the moonlight reflecting on the snow to help light the way and prevent her from falling. After a short while the man said "This is it" and they turned into a road with a row of houses. After consulting the address on the scrap of paper she found the correct building. With hope in her heart, she took a deep breath, walked up some steps and knocked on the door. A window on the first floor was flung open and a woman leant out asking what she wanted. "I'm looking for my mother, Maria Scheitza," Hildegard told her. The woman said "Well, she was staying here for a while but she moved." Hildegard's heart sank but then the woman told her not to worry as she had left a forwarding address and went to find it for her. Moments later the woman opened the door and handed Hildegard the new address that had been left for her by her mother.

The man had waited for her at the foot of the steps to the building and it seemed that he and his dog were going to stay with her until she found her family, so Hildegard showed him the new address which he recognised and off they set. In this strange town, late at night, in the darkness, with snow falling, she did not know how she'd have coped without this man's help. She even imagined he might be her guardian angel.

Whoever he was Hildegard was very grateful to him as he led her to the next address a few streets away. He waited while Hildegard walked up another set of steps to the door of the house and knocked. A lady opened the door and Hildegard explained who she was and that she believed her mother and sister were staying here. "Oh Hildegard!" she exclaimed, immediately reaching out in a big embrace. "Your mother will be so pleased to see you. She has been so worried about you, not even knowing if you were still alive. Please come in and I'll take you to her." Stepping over the threshold in relief, Hildegard remembered to look back half expecting the man to have disappeared, but he was still there so she was able to thank him for coming to her aid. He humbly responded that he was happy to have been of help before saying "Goodnight", and continuing on his way, leaving Hildegard wondering again if this man could possibly, in reality, be her guardian angel, if indeed an angel would be allowed to own a dog.

Hildegard, still bemused, became aware of the woman taking hold of her hand, and leading her down a corridor before knocking on one of the doors. The door was opened by a stunned

Maria, followed by Gretel both exclaiming 'Hilde!" Neither could believe their eyes. Hildegard, her mother and sister threw themselves into each other's arms and hugged and cried and cried and hugged. They were all speechless as not one of them could fully grasp the fact that they were actually together again. In Hildegard's own words "The joy was very great!" After so many months of not knowing if they would ever see each other again, months with no communication whatsoever, they all realised how blessed they were. So many were not so fortunate, having lost loved ones, homes, jobs and even their identities. But this family were so very grateful to have found each other.

The women had much news to share. Hildegard was glad to finally set down her rucksack, take off her coat and sit with her mother and sister to talk. Although she was more tired than she thought was possible, there was so much to tell and they talked and cried all night long. Hildegard told her mother and Gretel about Carlsbad and Anja and her job at the station, about the bombing and her decision to go home. She told of the impossibly long and treacherous journey on foot along the autobahn to get back to their village and about Peter and Else and how they brought her back to good health and then laying low in Peter's loft for months. She told them all about Jaginne and what she found there, the graves and sad losses of friends and family, of the changes there and the hardship. And then the perilous journey leaving Jaginne again and coming here to Neumark to find her dear family.

Her mother's hands clasped at her heart when she realised all the dangerous situations Hildegard had been in and the horrors of war, the loss of lives and destruction of property, including their own home. Maria told Hildegard that on arriving in Neumark she and Gretel stayed in a camp until they were both able to find jobs and were able to pay rent for a room. She had a job cleaning in a factory and Gretel found work in a tailoring shop. They earned very little and had coupons for food but it was never enough. The room they lived in had two beds and a small stove in the middle of the room. "Well today" announced Hildegard proudly, "We will eat well!" and out of her bag she pulled the rest of the bread and the smoked bacon Peter had given her. She had brought enough to last a few days. The family stopped talking and ate with relish. So happy to have food on the table, but mainly to be together again.

Hildegard stayed with her mother and sister in that one room for three months. She met many fellow refugees, some from neighbouring villages to Jaginne, who had found work in Neumark. All wanted to know what it was like at home. Some were happy to stay but others were desperate to return home. Hildegard and her family realised a decision needed to be made whether they should stay safely here in Germany or go back home to what was now Poland. Her mother was happy in this new town and felt safe. She had her job cleaning at the factory and Gretel enjoyed working in the tailor's shop doing something she loved. Should they risk going back to the sadness and destruction? Did they want to live under a Communist regime? There was so much to consider.

Hildegard herself had been unable to find a job in Neumark so money for food for the family was being stretched even more thinly. She discovered that her mother, whilst at work at the factory, would slip the occasional few of lumps of coal into her pocket to bring home for the stove. Money was that short.

For now, though, the joy of finding her family alive and well meant everything to Hildegard. All those months of worry and now they were together again. One evening she and Gretel decided to go out to a dance. Hildegard was wearing a new pair of shoes. The shoes she'd acquired from the deserted house. A frivolous non-essential that she had packed 'just in case'. And now she had an unexpected opportunity to actually wear them. The shoes had a tiny heel and were perfect for dancing. The sisters had a wonderful evening, loving the music and the dancing and having fun for the first time in a very long while. It was such a treat for the sisters to go out and enjoy themselves together again. Her beautiful new shoes added to Hildegard's happiness. She felt so proud of them. She was even asked to dance by a young man. After the dance Gretel scolded her sister "You were holding that boy a bit too close!" "No, no!" protested Hildegard. "It was because my shoes were hurting so much. I had to hold on to him!" The girls laughed and chatted about the evening all the way home.

In the spring there was a carnival in Neumark, the first since the beginning of the war. It was a happy time for the family as they enjoyed the food and beer whilst watching the parades with townspeople dressed in bright costumes. Everyone came out to enjoy the fun. A much-needed breath of fresh air after the many dismal months of war and lack and a welcome change to see lots of happy, smiling, relaxed people.

However, as the carnival left Neumark, Hildegard realised decisions had to be made. The family all agreed they liked the town and felt quite settled, but the question still remained: do they stay here in this one small room, or go home where they had a house and lots of space around them? Hopefully other neighbours would be going back and maybe life would get back to normal. Hildegard knew that Else would return. After hearing through the grapevine that the Red Army appeared to have completely retreated out of the area surrounding Jaginne, the news lessened the lingering fears of returning home. With this in mind, and added to the fact that she was unable to secure a job no matter how hard she tried, Hildegard said "Well we will have to make up our minds one way or the other!"

Chapter 37

Back Home to Jaginne

The many conversations about their village and the forest left the family pining for home. A much more important reason to return, however, was Josef. Although he was always in their thoughts, not one of them had been able to visit him for over a year. A decision was finally made. They simply must return home.

After resigning from jobs, making arrangements to leave and saying goodbye to friends, it was time to go. Money was pooled to pay for rail tickets and Hildegard, her mother and Gretel set off by train. No journey was easy by rail as so many railway stations had been bombed with reparations still in progress. It was many hours before they completed the 490km (300 mile) trip, finally arriving in Jaginne the following day.

Although Hildegard had warned them, her mother and Gretel were shocked by the devastation and saddened by the addition of so many graves. So different from the village they had left many months previously. As stoic as ever, the family decided to count their blessings. They had found each other and they were once again standing on what they felt was home soil. They were all determined to try to get back to normal hoping that the Communist government would not make life too difficult.

The presence of Polish Police was a reminder that their village was no longer in Germany but now a part of Poland. There were many changes the family would have to get used to.

Maria and her daughters excitedly arrived at their house but something didn't feel quite right. Suddenly, from around the side of the house, a young woman appeared carrying a basket of laundry. With looks of total surprise on everyone's faces, Hildegard recognised her as a daughter of her father's sister Maria. After they'd all recovered from the initial shock, enough to remember polite greetings, the four women talked. Gisela had married a Pole and the couple were therefore allowed to take their pick of any abandoned house which had been left after the forced evacuations. Believing that, after all this time the Scheitzas had gone for good, as with many others, she and her husband decided to move into the house. After all, the house and land had been a wedding gift to Josef and Maria from their mutual grandparents and they felt that keeping it in the family was the right thing to do. It was a great shock for Gisela to see Tante Maria and her cousins standing before her, obviously with the intention of returning to their home. After explaining the situation, she said she would speak to her husband and they would decide what to do.

Hildegard and her family had not expected this turn of events. However, the end of the war had changed everything for them. The sad truth was the redrawing of borders by Allied leaders and subsequent expulsions of Germans from now non-German soil had left the Scheitza family homeless. There was no hope of requisitioning any property now considered to be on Polish soil. Poles were allowed to commandeer any property deserted by German expellees and it would be officially handed over to them. Hildegard could see the distress on her mother's face and her own spirits sank as this complication seemed insurmountable. In the meantime, Hildegard, Maria and Gretel found a place to spend the night.

The next day, Gisela, accompanied by her husband, sought out the family. The husband was an ethnic Pole and as such was entitled to claim the house as his own residence. However, this very kind man had spoken to the authorities and, explaining to them that the Scheitza family were relatives, he received an agreement which allowed Maria, Hildegard and Gretel to legally reclaim their home. Although it appeared that now, under a Communist Government, they no longer owned the house itself, the family were extremely relieved and grateful to Gisela and her husband to allow them to move back in.

Hildegard was glad her mother and sister had not seen the house as it had been when she initially returned to Jaginne, with the smashed furniture, the broken door and the bullet holes. Peter had done a good job with the repairs. However, once Gisela and her husband had moved out, Mama set to with the cleaning and scrubbing of her home until she felt it was theirs again.

Men continued to drift back into the village mostly returning from internment or prisoner of war camps, but many did not return. Most of the young men Hildegard and Gretel knew who had been sent to the Front did not come back. However, thankfully for Gretel she was able to welcome home her dear friend Erich who lived in a neighbouring village. He was one of the few to return safely and was relatively unscathed.

The three women continued to work tirelessly over the following weeks to completely restore their home and surrounding land in an attempt to bring it back to the condition it was before the evacuations. They somehow managed to retrieve their goat and find some furniture.

The entire eastern territories were now under Communism, so nobody owned anything nor were they able to earn much money. Everything belonged to the Government. Gretel took a job at the local mill and Hildegard worked in the village shop, but it was still hard to get by.

As with the returning neighbours, they did all they could to make the best of a bad situation. Else Jakubik along with her mother and her younger sister, were among those who had returned.

Sometimes a dance would be arranged, occasionally in Jaginne but mostly in Carlsruhe or Damratsch and friends from the village would gather together and make their way on foot to the dance. Gretel had got to know Erich Kuklok a little better and she would go with him. Hildegard's dancing partner was Willi Wabele. It was good to go out and enjoy themselves. However, their fun was often short lived due to the Polish Police who would be at every function to ensure there was no trouble. Instead of keeping the peace they would drink too much and wanted to dance with the prettiest girls. If anyone got in their way they would start shooting. Usually at the end of the dance there would be a brawl of some kind followed by shooting and the evening would be ruined.

Chapter 38

Restlessness

Although so very happy to be reunited with her family, and life together resumed in their family home, Hildegard soon became restless as she could not see a future for herself in Jaginne. She was unable to find any well-paid work. Gainful employment was very hard to come by. There was no possibility of returning to either of her previous jobs. Carlsruhe Station had been bombed towards the end of the war and was still under repair. Oppeln Station was fully operational and as busy as ever, with thousands of displaced people travelling to find loved ones or relocating, but as she had left her bicycle in Carlsbad, she had no means of travelling there and back and would not be able to afford to rent a room. She was therefore having to think carefully about what she should do next.

Meanwhile Gretel was regularly going out on dates with Erich Kuklok and seemed besotted with him. Eric, a farmer's son, worked on the family farm and had a good life but Hildegard felt he wasn't good enough for her sister. "But I love him!" Gretel would say in response to any challenging remarks from Hildegard.

With nothing to do and nothing to look forward to, Hildegard had to give serious consideration to her future. The simple yet happy quality of life in her home village had completely changed due to Russian occupation and Communism. Everything came under the control of the Government and there was a sense of general unhappiness and discontent. During the war all bank and savings accounts had been claimed for the war effort. What hope was there for her in and around Jaginne?

Hildegard had heard nothing from her friend Karl for a couple of years now and she feared the worst. He had either been killed or he had found someone else. Her initial contentment of finding her family and being back in their home, was waning.

Gretel was busy with her dressmaking, and she now had a job in a kindergarten. Most of her spare time was spent with Erich. Else was now engaged to be married. Her Polish fiancé had been released from the work camp, had returned to the village and they were now planning their wedding. Other friends had resigned themselves to the situation, deciding to make the best of it.

If she had a better-paid job it might be different. She needed to work. She needed to fill her days usefully and be self-sufficient or at least add to the family income. Everyone around her seemed just content to be home with no ambition for a better life. Both her best friend and her sister were looking forward to marriage and a future with their husbands-to-be.

Hildegard had seen and experienced life outside of Jaginne. Big towns and cities with more to see and do and more opportunities. She had met many different and interesting people and felt she had experienced a little more of the world. After all she had been through she had no fear of going away again. It was with these thoughts in her mind that she knew she had to leave.

Before she made any arrangements Hildegard ensured she visited her father in the hospital. Knowing his family were back in the family home, he wanted to be there too. Maria wasn't too sure. She knew it would be very hard for her as her husband needed lots of care due to his condition. She would have to watch him constantly and she felt that was just not possible with all the work she had to do both in the house and on the land. However, she missed Josef. They'd been parted for 12 years and, despite his disabilities, she came to the conclusion that she wanted him home. It was agreed that, as soon as the house was properly repaired and re-organised, he could return. This made Josef very happy and Hildegard too as Mama would now not be left alone due to both daughters planning to fly the nest.

Chapter 39

At Last, News of Karl

As the workings of practical life in war torn Europe began to very slowly return to normal, the postal service was resumed and people were able to more easily try and make contact with scattered or missing loved ones. One day in May 1946, a few weeks after returning home to Jaginne, out of the blue came a letter from Oncle Hans in Berlin with news of Karl. Hildegard had given him her uncle's address in case he couldn't track her down and he had written to Oncle Hans asking him to let his niece know that he was alive and well. Oncle Hans was happy to pass this information to Hildegard by letter to tell her the good news and report that, whilst fighting in Holland two years previously, Karl had been captured by American Forces and had been transported to America as a Prisoner of War. Oncle Hans had enclosed Karl's address for Hildegard to respond, and she did so immediately. She was so happy to hear he was safe and immediately wrote to Karl to let him know where and how she was and to tell him briefly what had been happening to her and her family since their last letters.

Karl replied straight away and explained more about his current situation. Before his capture, he had been part of a defence strategy which was trying to prevent Holland from being occupied by British, French and American Allies. After being transported to America, he had been sent to a prison camp on the east coast and later to a camp in Alabama to work on a sugar plantation. He was glad to say he had no complaints regarding his time in America as a Prisoner of War. Unlike PoW's captured by Nazi armies he was treated very well. He also admitted that he was glad to have been taken far away from the conflict and the hardship.

Karl really liked America and decided he'd like to live there. He told Hildegard that he would like her to join him and start a new life together there. However, he had looked into getting her the necessary papers and found it was not a possibility due to the fact they weren't married. Karl had no desire to return to Germany partly due to the fact he had no real family there. He hoped Hildegard was waiting for him, but his future was uncertain. Would she agree to leave her family and Germany? Hildegard told her mother and Gretel. "But America is too far away Hilde! Please don't go!" cried Mama. "I will never see you again!" So, although the offer was very tempting, as life in America sounded quite wonderful, Hildegard wrote back to Karl explaining her dilemma.

Karl replied saying he understood but as Hildegard's family were unhappy for her to go to America, he would return to Germany for her but he needed to continue to work to save money for his fare. He also sent a package as a surprise. She excitedly opened it to find the most wonderful gifts. There were nylons, a beautiful scarf, a pair of leather boots and, several smaller items. She was so happy and her mother and Gretel were pleased that the gifts had lifted her spirits. There was a dance the next evening and Hildegard proudly wore her new boots and scarf. After explaining to her friends at the dance how she had acquired her new apparel, they teased her saying "Boyfriend in America! Oooo!".

Despite the fun evening with her friends, inside Hildegard was frustrated and confused. She had no idea how Karl's plans would work out. Would he be able to save enough money to leave America for her? How long would it all take? Would a future life with Karl work out as she hoped?

All these concerns did not solve her immediate problem so she made a decision. She would head north towards Berlin and find work. She would not be alone in Berlin as Oncle Hans and his family would not be too far away if she needed them.

Once again Hildegard packed her bags and, much to the dismay of her mother and sister, in June 1946 she said fond farewells to family and friends and prepared for yet another adventure. At least this time she felt relatively safe. Her mother found the parting hard wondering if Hildegard would ever return.

"You'll come back, won't you?" asked Maria hopefully. Hildegard responded by first hugging her mother tightly and then her sister saying "I hope so." She quickly turned to hide her tears and walked away towards the neighbour's truck which was waiting to take her on a journey towards what she hoped would be a new and happy future.

Part Ten

1946 - 1949

Chapter 40

East Berlin and the Garden Shop

Travelling to the outskirts of Berlin did not pose a problem. Although papers needed to be regularly shown, Hildegard was able to take a train which took her across the Polish border into East Germany and to East Berlin, all being occupied by the Soviet Military.

Once in East Berlin Hildegard found a camp where she could stay until she found a job. Like the camps in Carlsbad, many of them were initially built across the country for Military use. Before and during the Second World War, tens of thousands more were built and all utilised for the internment of millions of dissenters, prisoners of war, or Jews, where they were places of cruelty, torture, deprivation and violence. Post war, the camps were now proving useful for the temporary housing of the homeless of the locality as well as for displaced German refugees forced from their homelands in the East. The camp in which Hildegard now found herself had been a purpose-built barracks and, although in very bad repair, it was clean and she was given her own room.

As soon as she had unpacked and settled into her accommodation, Hildegard took a trip into Berlin itself to find it was not the beautiful city she remembered as a child when visiting Oncle Hans with her father. The city had been hit excessively by Allied air raids as well as retaliating attacks by Soviets. Much work had already been carried out to clear the bomb damage which had resulted in huge piles of rubble lining the Berlin streets. Due to the lack of fighting aged men, the work had mainly been carried out by women, old and young, who had spent hours filling wheel barrows and transporting debris to fill in bomb craters. Even now the clean-up job continued as Berliners tried to put their city back together again.

Berlin was now divided; West Berlin being equally occupied by British, French and American troops, with Russia occupying East Berlin which was now under Communist rule.

There was very little money and also little food. Conditions were worse in East Berlin due to Communism and Soviet rule which continued to punish native Germans for the annihilation of millions of their countrymen.

As camps became overcrowded, Berliners were ordered to take in expellees as tens of thousands continued to pour into the city. A family would be required to share a bedroom whilst refugees had the remaining rooms whilst sharing the kitchen, bathroom and toilet facilities.

Hildegard, in her quest to earn money, thankfully found a job in a *Gartenladen* (Garden Shop, or Garden Centre) run by Herr and Frau Engelmann. Although she missed her family, she was determined to make the most of her time away and approach this new phase of her life with positivity. Tasks in her new job included the planting and picking of fruits and vegetables and she quickly made a good friend of one of the employees, a younger girl called Erika.

Food shortages and the economy meant that most Berliners had no choice but to survive on 800 calories per day. Hildegard wondered if she'd made the right decision coming all this way just to be starved. But she decided to make the best of it. The two young women would sometimes go out together to find food to eat and other times they would eat in the large kitchen at the shop. It was good to have a friend to spend time with.

Hildegard enjoyed meeting new people and getting to know them. Whilst working at the Garden Shop she met a wounded soldier and enjoyed listening to his stories. The soldier somehow had access to extra bread rations, more than likely illegally, and he would often bring her some of his haul. The owners of the Garden Shop would ask Hilde "Were do you get your bread?" She would answer "Oh someone had it left over and gave it to me." Everyone was hungry. No one had enough to eat and therefore Hildegard did not think it wise to divulge her source.

As well as indoor and outdoor plants the Garden Shop grew and sold a variety of fruits and vegetables, a main crop of which being tomatoes. The owners would provide lunch for their workers, tomato soup being a popular choice. In fact, almost always the sole choice was tomato soup. It would be true to say there was always tomato soup, and very little else. Hildegard and Erika would joke that they were up to their necks in tomato soup! So much so that Hildegard often suffered from stomach ache. Each week they would buy a small piece butter with their coupons to spread on their bread to help the tomato soup go down. Food was very important to Hildegard as it seemed she had been hungry for a very long time – at least since the expulsions. There had been many times she could honestly say that she'd been starving. Hildegard and Erica were grateful to their employers and very occasionally they would gather and save enough food to cook something a little different and invite them to eat lunch with them in the shop kitchen.

During her time in Berlin, Hildegard regularly exchanged letters with her mother and sister. Shortly after her departure her mother, as hoped, arranged for her father to come home. It was not easy for Maria as Josef was not the strong and able man he was before but she was very happy to have him back in the family home, especially in the absence of her rock, Hildegard.

Meanwhile Hildegard and Karl continued to write to each other as Karl tried to save enough money to leave America. He was definite about not wanting to return to Germany. He eventually found a ship bound for England, the Captain of which agreed he could pay for his passage by working on board. Karl had a good friend in England who he had kept in touch with. He and Walter first met and became friends in Stuttgart in their youth and they joined the German Army together aged 17. Walter had been captured by the British Army and sent to a PoW camp in Folkstone. Therefore, on arriving in England, Karl headed for Dymchurch in Kent where Walter had worked since his release. After finding his friend, Karl wrote to Hildegard to tell her he had found a job working on a farm in Lydd, Romney Marsh on the English south coast. His intention was to establish himself in England and earn some money and, when settled a little, he would come to meet her in Germany.

Hildegard wondered in all reality if she would ever see Karl again. She couldn't be sure as his plans seemed very complicated and unlikely. He may meet someone in England and marry. Her future was far from clear. She decided not to think about it too much and just keep busy.

Occasionally at the weekends Hildegard would take the train to visit her relatives. She especially enjoyed her visits with Oncle Hans and Tante Anna at their *Schrebergarten* outside of the city. The *Schrebergarten* or Schreiber Garden project was named after German physician Moritz Schreiber who specialised in children's health. In 1864 he introduced small gardens on the outskirts of Berlin for children to tend with their parents for the good of their health and wellbeing. Also known as the *Kleinegarten* (*s*mall garden), the idea grew and plots of unused land around most German cities and along railway lines were rented to those living in apartments to turn the plots into allotment gardens so they could enjoy fresh air and outdoor life. There would be strict measurements taken and equally strict rules and regulations were laid down. Each garden would be fenced in and not exceed 400sq metres. It was permissible and usual for a summerhouse to be built on the plot with the size not exceeding 24sq metres. The gardens would be carefully laid out to include various fresh fruit and vegetable plots but it was also important to create a garden to relax in with flowers and trees and somewhere to sit. Although it was not permitted to live full time in the little houses on the plots, tenants would often equip them with beds and a small kitchen area so they could at least spend the weekends there.

Oncle Hans still worked at the large department store in Berlin and he and his family lived in an apartment nearby, so their escapes to their garden on summer evenings and weekends were important to them. Hildegard was able to make many visits to the garden during her time in Berlin and would look forward to and enjoy a homecooked meal which always included their home-grown fruits and vegetables. Oncle Hans and his wife claimed the garden had kept them safe and alive as they were able to escape there during the bombings and attacks on Berlin during the war. Schrebergartens were also lauded for saving many German city dwellers from malnourishment and starvation during the war thanks to the opportunity to grow much of their own food.

Chapter 41

The Bakery

The winter of 1946 went down in history as one of the coldest on record. Accommodation for Berliners was scant due to the bombing and destruction of homes. Waterways bringing fuel and food to the city were frozen over. Due to the frugal conditions, teamed with extreme temperatures which had dropped to 25 degrees below freezing, thousands were dying from the cold as the horrendous situation became known as The White Death.

Along with visits to see her Oncle, Hildegard was grateful for her job at the Garden Shop which at least provided some food and for the camp that gave her a roof over her head. But after working outside in the fields through the long freezing winter, and now suffering from acute back pain, by the spring of 1947 she felt enough was enough and decided it was time to search for another, less labour intensive, means of earning money.

Before too long Hildegard came across a vacancy sign in the window of a Bakery which she felt fit the requirements of a hungry refugee perfectly. The fact that the position came with a room made the decision to accept the job an easy one. However, as time progressed the reality was not as she had anticipated. Hildegard expected she'd have the pick of the shop's selection of bread and cakes and that, at last, she would experience a full stomach. Unfortunately, this was not the case as the owners were very strict and locked everything away. If she wanted a bread roll she had to pay for it. The owners were far from generous she decided. Even the owner's grandfather, who also stayed with them, complained he was constantly hungry.

In addition to the bakery, the owners also possessed a number of adjacent fields and barns and very soon into her new position Hildegard learned she was to rise at 5 am each morning to help milk the cow, clean out the barn and replace with fresh hay before being sent out to work in the fields. Things were not working out at all as she expected. It was extremely difficult and heavy work and no matter how hard she tried she could only ever get a few drops of milk from the cow. The baker's wife was not pleased. "You're no good", she said. "You will have to work in the house and in the shop." Hildegard stifled a huge sigh of relief. Working in the house and shop would suit her much better.

Chapter 42

Frau Nutschke and a Job in a Hotel

Although glad to be finally working inside, after persevering with her rather grumpy boss for a few more months, early in 1948 Hildegard decided to continue her search for a more suitable job. She eventually came across an advertisement for a position in a Hotel in Glienick, a pretty rural town on the edge of the town of Zossen, South Berlin. The owner Frau Nutschke was all alone and, as her husband was still in captivity, she desperately needed help in the hotel's restaurant. Hildegard was provided with a room of her own, loved the work and got to know lots of young people. She felt that she had finally found a job she actually enjoyed.

Sometimes a dance would be organised at the Hotel which Hildegard would attend. During these evenings, as the band played, for a while all her worries and concerns for the future seemed to disappear.

Frau Nitschke was a kind woman and occasionally she would arrange a meeting at the Hotel for refugees. Companies and individuals would donate clothing and these would be made available to those in need. Hildegard was happy to have something different to wear and, although the clothes weren't always to her taste, she accepted them gratefully.

As time passed, Herr Nutschke was finally released and able to come home, but he was not a well man. Hildegard was glad to be able to continue to contribute in some way to support Frau Nutschke.

On her days off, as well as her occasional visits to Oncle Hans at his Schrebergarten, Hildegard would travel by train to visit Tante Sopfie, her father's sister. Tante Sopfie had moved to Berlin after leaving school and found work on a large nursery that supplied various businesses in Berlin with fruits and vegetables. She fell in love with the rich land owner and they married and had a family. Tante Sopfie would sometimes invite Hildegard to their house at weekends. She would look forward to the visits as there would always be a warm welcome and a good meal waiting for her. She was grateful to have family an easy distance away.

Hildegard eventually grew accustomed to the bleak quality of life of East Germany under Soviet rule and Communism. Now 3 years since the end of the war, life in West Germany, with the help of the Allies, was improving. Cities were being rebuilt but as the Deutsche Mark had lost its value and was worthless, shops were still closed and people were still bartering for goods. The Allied powers, who were working hard to clean up Hitler's mess in the country, arranged for the development of a new Deutsche Mark which was launched in West Berlin on 20th June 1948. Suddenly the city's shop windows were full and West Berliners found they could purchase everything they needed. There were great celebrations.

Naturally this turn of fortune pleased the resident West Berliners no end but it was too much for the Soviet Union who still held all Germans in contempt. They should still be suffering for their grave sins towards Russia during the war, not celebrating. Stalin in his anger ordered the Red Army to close all checkpoints thereby stopping all food, coal and other goods from entering the city. They also cut off all electricity, leaving West Berlin in the dark as well as cold and hungry, mirroring life in the east.

In the United States, President Truman was alerted to this dilemma and, as well as getting aid to the suffering Berliners, he had to alleviate the risk of Berlin falling. The only possible and legal way to get goods into the city was by air so he organised for hundreds of US Military aircraft to fly over the city dropping food and coal. It was a huge operation. The airlifts into West Berlin, after perfecting this remarkable humanitarian plan, comprised 700 flights carrying 5000 tons of goods, daily!

A US airman, seeing children line up to watch the air drops, decided the young needed an occasional treat so he began to drop little parachutes containing chocolate and sweets and gum he'd bought with his rations. These special drops provided the children with such excitement and fun that he encouraged his fellow airmen to do the same and many children were able to enjoy these precious gifts falling from the sky. The airmen, seeing the smiles on the children's faces, felt those in East Berlin deserved some happiness too so made a plan to drop the little parachutes over the border as well. Of course, none of these good will gestures were going to please Stalin in the middle of his war with the west and so, after a mini parachute drop of chocolate and sweets was made into East Berlin, Russia sent a stern warning to President Truman, causing the children of East Berlin to have to do without.

 It took a year before Stalin was able to admit he was beaten in his efforts to punish West Berliners and reopened the checkpoints. The event solidified relations between the Allies and the German people. Kindness, thoughtfulness and freedom had won the day.

Chapter 43

A Life Changing Letter

Meanwhile, in the autumn of 1948, as Hildegard continued to work hard for Frau Nutschke, whilst making the best of life in the cold, dark and bleak conditions of East Berlin, out of the blue she received a letter from Karl. He announced he was taking 2 weeks leave, and after visiting what little family he had left in Stuttgart in West Germany, he would be in nearby Goppingen before Christmas with the aim of taking her back to England with him.

Hildegard was shocked. After all this time waiting and wondering if they would ever be together, the time was suddenly here. There was a lot to arrange so she immediately set about the difficult task of obtaining a visa to travel to England. Karl hadn't given her very much time and with such short notice this proved to be impossible.

Hildegard wrote to Karl explaining that she wasn't able to arrange the necessary paperwork to travel to England. She begged him to cross the border and meet her in East Germany but he declined, saying he would be arrested and probably shot as unwelcome by Soviet Police. He insisted it would be easier for her to cross the border into West Germany. Hildegard realised the enormous danger for Karl so agreed that she would attempt to cross. Karl had contacts who gave instructions of where she needed to go and Karl passed these to Hildegard along with the name of a man who would help her.

Hildegard spoke to both Oncle Hans and Tante Sopfie who warned her not to go. She asked for their financial help as she may need to bribe a guard but they refused, considering it madness to try and cross the border. They warned her that many people attempting to cross had been either imprisoned or shot. They could not assist her attempt to make such a dangerous trip.

She asked Frau Nutschke who also refused. In fact, she kept back her pay to prevent her from going.

Hildegard needed to be alone so that she could think it through and make up her mind what to do so she went to the church and prayed. After praying she believed she knew what she had to do. She had decided. She wanted a better life and it was therefore worth the risk to try and cross the border.

The day approached and Hildegard packed her suitcase, dressed in her warmest clothes, put all the money she had in her purse and took a train on that cold December day to the village that Karl had indicated in his letter. The village was situated next to the checkpoint on the outskirts of Berlin and on arrival, without bringing attention to herself, she was to search for the man Karl had said would help her. He would be drinking in a certain bar not far from the checkpoint. This man had helped many cross the border and she had to find him.

It was a cold night and snow was falling but thankfully Hildegard had little trouble locating the establishment. On entering the noisy bar, she cast her eyes over the smoke-filled room and the sea of people gathered there. Mostly men and some women, the men holding their steins of beer. It was far from obvious, amongst all of these people, who exactly might be the man she was seeking. She moved through the throng of people asking some did they know this man, but no one could help her, perhaps fearful of being seen aiding and abetting. Then finally she found someone who was willing to point him out to her.

Hildegard approached the man who was sitting on a high stool at the bar, hunched over his beer and said "I believe you help people cross the border. Can you please help me?" "Hmmm … are you asking me to put my life in danger as well as yours?" he asked. But after careful consideration he at length muttered quietly "OK". "The Russians at the border have fierce guard dogs. The only time I would be willing to take you would be in the evening after the dogs have eaten and they are tired and sleepy. It will also be the guards' break and they will be drinking vodka so that's the best time." Hildegard immediately agreed and gave him the money she had saved. "Meet me here at 5.30 this evening and I'll show you the way. But there will be no talking. We will walk in silence." And then he was gone.

At precisely 5.30pm Hildegard found herself walking along a dark snow-covered street towards a man who she didn't know but in whom she was putting her trust. He silently took hold of her suitcase and together they made their way towards the checkpoint. There was no sound as they walked across the blanket of soft snow. All was quiet and still when they arrived at 6pm.

The man had obviously done this before. As hoped for, the dogs had obviously been fed as they were nowhere to be seen. The Russian guards were otherwise engaged and there were none in sight. The pair passed quickly through the checkpoint and began the long walk to the West. After 2km the man whispered, "This is as far as I go. You are now on no man's land. See that small light in the distance? That's the West. Just keep walking. Good luck and say your prayers." He handed her the suitcase and he was gone. Hildegard did as she was told and, not taking her eyes off the small light, she walked and prayed "Please God don't let the Russians see me". She was petrified but she'd come this far and there was no turning back.

Due to the lack of street lighting in Communist East Germany, people were used to the pitch black as soon as night fell. With darkness all around her, Hildegard kept her eyes on the small light. She walked as fast as she could down the endless road, the ever-growing light in the distance encouraging her. The further she walked the bigger the light became, until eventually the brightness became so blinding that she couldn't see clearly. As her eyes became accustomed, she realised she had come to the end of the road and light was all around her. A car drew up as if from nowhere and she jumped with fright. It was a police vehicle. She froze. Then a loud voice shouted in German, "*Halt, Fraulein! Wo gehst du hin*? (Stop Miss! Where are you going?)" Hildegard felt sick. "This is it! It's over. They will either shoot me or send me to prison!" She took a deep breath and somehow found her voice, saying "I'm going to see my boyfriend!" Then the surprise reply, "Don't be afraid. You're safe now. You are in the West!" Hildegard was speechless as relief washed over her. She could have cried but gulped back the tears as the German policeman immediately directed her to a small hotel where she could get some food and stay overnight.

Hildegard was surprised to see there were already a number of people there, young and old, who had also just crossed the border to this transition point. As she chatted to some it seemed that most had crossed over to find someone – family members, children, prisoners of war. Everyone had a story to tell but Hildegard was too tired to share at this point and just wanted to sleep. Tomorrow was another day with, no doubt, problems of its own.

Chapter 44

A Necessary Trip to Wolfsburg

After a fitful night's sleep, Hildegard rose in the morning to try to work out what to do next. She had successfully crossed the border but Karl had told her he would meet her in Goppingen. Goppingen was over 600km away and she did not have enough Deutsche Marks. She felt completely deflated as the situation seemed hopeless. As her mind searched for a solution, she remembered that an old friend she knew from Jaginne, Cilla Kopka, had told her that her sister Helene and her husband had decided, after the expulsions, to make a new life for themselves in Wolfsburg which was not too far away. Cilla had given Hildegard her sister's address in case she needed it. If only she could get there she felt sure they would help her. She didn't know her married name but she knew that her husband worked at the Volkswagen car factory. Hildegard packed her bags and made her way to the railway station to see if she had enough money to purchase a ticket to Wolfsburg. To her astonishment and relief, she found she had just enough.

The two-hour journey was straightforward and Hildegard hoped that Helene, known by family and friends as Lene, was at home. On arrival at Wolfsburg Station, Hildegard asked at the ticket office for directions to Lene's address and found it easily. On arrival she knocked tentatively at the door and it was opened by a shocked Lene who exclaimed "Hilde! I can't believe it's you! Come in out of the cold! What are you doing here?" The young women were so pleased to see each other again and after Lene provided Hildegard with hot soup and drink, they sat and chatted, sharing their experiences since that fateful February night almost 4 years before when they and their fellow villagers were forced to evacuate their homes. Lene now had a little boy and she and her family were very happy in Wolfsburg. They were doing well as her husband's job enabled them to live in this nice apartment and they had even bought a car. Between them they shared information on who was back home in Jaginne and who had decided to make new lives for themselves in West Germany. They also shared their sadness for those who didn't make it and their families.

Hildegard told Lene her story and plucked up the courage to ask her if she could borrow some money which she would pay back as soon as she could. She told her of her boyfriend Karl and how he had been captured and taken as a Prisoner of War to America and how, as she wouldn't go to America, he had eventually been able to travel England and find employment there and the papers needed to go to England were much easier to obtain. She explained how he was on a two-week holiday from his job and she had got this far but had now run out of money for the final part of the journey to Goppingen. Lene felt very sorry for her friend and, as it was only natural to help a fellow villager in need, it was easy for her to agree. "Of course, Hilde. We would be glad to help. We know you, trust you and care about you so we have no qualms in lending you what you need."

Karl had given Hildegard a contact telephone number of where he was staying so Lene took her to the nearby post office where she could make the call. Hildegard eventually got through to Karl and they arranged to meet the next day at the railway station in Goppingen.

Lene and her husband invited Hildegard to stay the night and the next morning they drove her to the station. After helping with her luggage Lene's husband found out the times of trains and connections.

"Thank you" said Hildegard, as she boarded the train. "I promise to pay back every penny as soon as possible!" After she'd waved them goodbye and stacked her luggage, she sat down and kicked off her boots, overwhelmed with gratitude for her friends' kindness and relief that her problems had been resolved. She could now relax for a few hours on the journey and not worry. The loan from her friends was an answer to prayer.

After a while the train pulled in to a station and all the passengers were suddenly on their feet delving into coat pockets and bags for papers. It appeared that they had arrived at a British/American border and personal identification and other paperwork needed to be shown. Military Personnel boarded the train and checked everyone's papers. Hildegard was unaware this was going to happen and did not have the necessary paperwork. It was obvious that others were in the same situation. "Everyone without travel permits off the train!" shouted one of the Military. Hildegard and all those alighting the train were led to a large room where they were told in no uncertain terms that they were not permitted to travel further and that they were all to return to the Russian zone which was back over the border into East Germany.

Now what should she do? After risking her life getting across from the East to West Germany is this really as far as she could go? She wanted to cry but instead decided to pray. Hildegard then remembered the telephone number. She found a public telephone and thankfully got through to Karl. He told her all was not lost and gave her instructions of another way to get to him but as it was clear that she wouldn't arrive till very late that day, they agreed to meet the next day instead.

Hildegard was determined. She'd taken huge risks to come this far and she wasn't going to let a small thing like Border Police get in the way of her meeting with Karl. She had put all her hopes for her future life in him. He had promised her so much and she was not about to throw that away. Following Karl's instructions, she started to walk as if returning to where she came from, for the sake of the Border Police. She found somewhere to stay overnight and the next day she doubled back and found a way to enter the American zone without going through a check point. From here she was able to board another train going to Goppingen. She sat back on the train bench and sighed and prayed "Please God, my nerves are jangling. Please don't let there be any more problems".

Chapter 45

Reuniting with Karl

A few hours later, on her arrival at Goppingen Station, Hildegard climbed down the steps of the train and there was Karl standing on the platform waiting for her. They were meeting face to face for the first time in five long years. In her own words she said "The happiness was very great. I couldn't even describe it! We were both full of joy and laughter that we were finally together." Sadly though, his two weeks' leave had come to an end and Karl had to return to England the very next day. He was working under contract and had no choice. The couple had just a few hours to spend with each other at the station, enjoying each other's company and making plans for the future. Hildegard was distraught that Karl had to leave her again but he promised that between them they would organise all the necessary papers she needed for her passage to England and assured her that she wouldn't have to wait too long. Hildegard wasn't sure if she would like England and voiced her concerns, so they made a plan to live and work together there for a year and then see how she felt. She agreed that was a good idea and was more than happy to try.

The immediate problem for Hildegard was that she had arrived in a strange town in West Germany with no job and no lodgings and she didn't know what to do. Thankfully Karl had thought of this and had arranged for her to stay with a family he knew in the town.

After fond but reluctant farewells, Hildegard made her way to the home of Frau Bauerle and family. The address was easy to find and, as the lady of her new temporary residence opened the door, her spirits were lifted as Frau Bauerle greeted her warmly.

Chapter 46

The Bauerle Family

Frau Bauerle made Hildegard feel very welcome. She said "I know what you are going through." Hildegard was surprised to hear that Frau Bauerle and her three children were refugees from South Africa. They'd had a good life there. Her husband had been a successful businessman in their home country and they had a large property with many staff and workers. Though many South Africans were Germanic through their birth lines, at the beginning of the war South Africa made the decision to join the Allies and to fight Hitler. Frau Bauerle explained that many of the population were in opposition to this. Also, at this time, came the rise of apartheid. Up to this point South Africa's main industry was gold and mining but the war years created the need for the manufacture of war related supplies. As many workers had been called up to join the Army, factories depended on women workers but the workforce wasn't large enough. This resulted in a huge surge of North Africans coming into the country to take up the jobs and taking up residence in large ghettos outside of the cities. Unrest between the races started to grow and, though Frau Bauerle couldn't tell Hildegard more than that, she did tell her that her husband was shot and Frau Bauerle, fearful for her safety and that of her children, felt she had no choice but to flee and take refuge in the country of their ancestors.

In post war Goppingen she and her children were safe. Though this refugee family had only two rooms to live in, they were more than happy to have Hildegard stay for a while and help her settle into this unfamiliar town. Frau Bauerle was sympathetic to Hildegard's situation and was more than willing to sacrifice her family's comfort for a while in order to give her a place to stay until she found alternative lodgings.

The Bauerles were very nice compassionate people who had been through a lot. The two sons were old enough to go to work and the daughter, Meta, was continuing with her education. They all spoke English so Hildegard tried to pick up some of the language. She was very happy to stay here until her papers came through.

Meanwhile Karl was back in England and he and Hildegard continued to communicate by letter. Hildegard realised she would have to find a job as she couldn't live with the Bauerle family for too long for free but even to be allowed to work she needed a passport and the correct papers. In order to have the necessary paperwork drawn up with a new passport she needed to answer lots of questions, sit an examination and stay at one address for a period of time. In addition, whatever she needed, due to her refugee status, as well as lack of work and money, she had to join a queue for. For food, for blankets, for towels and other necessities.

The legal documents she needed were not going to be sorted out quickly so Hildegard did all she could to help Frau Bauerle. She would help with household chores, cleaning and shopping. It was so kind of her host to make such a huge sacrifice for her.

Hildegard liked Goppingen which was situated in the Stuttgart Region of Baden-Wurttemberg. Though bombed quite heavily towards the end of the war due to its Military airfield, it was a beautiful city. These days West and East Germany bore no resemblance to each other. Here in the West food and other necessities were becoming more plentiful and streets were lit at night. Also making life better for German citizens was the Allied occupation. In Goppingen the United States Army was there to help the people and the country to heal and return to a better way of life.

After staying with the Bauerle family for a few weeks Hildegard's passport and necessary documents came through which enabled her to look for work. She soon found a family in need of help which included looking after their 4-year-old daughter. It was time to say very sad goodbyes to Frau Bauerle and her family and thank them for their kindness.

Chapter 47

The Staudenmayers

Herr and Frau Staudenmayer owned a nice house and ran a business together. As well as taking care of their daughter Suzie and taking her to and from kindergarten, Hildegard helped out in the house.

The Staudenmayer's business was in the creation of cut-glass items mostly decorated with grapes and other patterns. Hildegard was occasionally able to go into the workshop to watch the process. A man came once a week to work on the designs which required a steady hand and extreme precision to prevent the glass from breaking. Hildegard found it fascinating to watch and appreciated the skill needed to produce these items of beauty.

The family treated Hildegard very well and the work was easy. The weather in the summer of 1949 was particularly good. On Sundays the family would take a ride through the stunning Goppingen countryside and high up into the beautiful and historic Staufen Park with its walking trails, picnic spots and lake. Hildegard would sit in the sunshine amongst the apple trees and gaze upon the sheep in the meadows and the river below. Here in the warmth and peace, whilst overlooking the most wonderful scenery, she would write to Karl.

Around this time Hildegard's sister Gretel married Erich Kuklok in Jaginne, the name of their village having been given the new Polish name of Jagienna. Gretel wrote and told her all about the wedding and promised to send photographs. Everyone was there - except her sister. Hildegard was filled with sadness as she imagined this happy occasion attended by all their friends and family, while she was so far away from everyone she loved. She was pleased for Gretel and Erich and hoped they had a long and happy married life together.

Meanwhile Hildegard had no family and no boyfriend, just the hope that Karl would send for her and provide for her the new life he had promised and that she dreamed of. However, the longer time went on the more she realised she had no guarantees this would happen.

Hildegard enjoyed living in Goppingen so much that in a letter to Karl she asked if he would come to Germany and make this lovely town their home. But Karl convinced her by reiterating "Come to England for one year and, if you don't like it, we will come back." Karl was now working as a groundsman for the owners of a bit house near Woking in Surrey, England and the job of housekeeper was waiting for Hildegard. In their kindness the owners also offered to pay her fare of £12 to England with a view to Karl repaying them weekly from his wages.

Chapter 48

Time to Leave

After almost a year in Goppingen, summer turned to autumn and in October 1949 Hildegard finally received all the papers, passport and entry permit for her to leave for England.

The time had finally come. Hildegard was to leave for a new life in another country. After packing her bags, she tearfully said goodbye to her friends in Goppingen who had done so much to help and support her.

Thankfully the weather was good which helped on this incredibly long passage from Germany to England. The first leg for Hildegard was the 7-hour train journey from Goppingen to *Koln* (Cologne). From *Koln* a 6-hour train journey took her to the port in Holland where she boarded a boat for Dover. Many on the 8-hour journey were seasick, including Hildegard.

Epilogue

1949 To England

Chapter 49

A New Life in England

In Hildegard's own words:

"*By the time I arrived in London, I had been travelling for two days. Karl was there to meet me at Liverpool Street Station. The joy was enormous. We had a lot to talk about.*

"*We took the train to West Byfleet in Surrey where Karl's employer's wife, picked us up in her car. I spoke no English so Karl had to translate at first whilst I learned the language.*

"*It was so wonderful to be here in England after the long war and my wanderings in Germany. I wrote to my mother and Gretel and later sent them parcels with items they couldn't buy in East Germany.*

"*Whilst Karl rented a room in nearby Woking and worked part time as groundsman in the big house, I was employed as a housekeeper with lodgings included. It was a big house with 9 bedrooms, 3 bathrooms and a big garden. At first, I imagined everyone in England was very rich and lived in houses like this.*

"*The lady of the house helped run the local Women's Institute group. I crocheted a waistcoat for her. I don't know if she kept it for herself or put in in the WI sale.*

"*During this time, I learned to cook popular English dishes such as Yorkshire pudding. It was good to have plenty to eat after the wartime rationing.*

"*A sister of the owner was a teacher and she helped me learn some English at the beginning so that I understood the most important things. Everyone was helpful and patient with me as I learned the language.*

"*I came to England with very few clothes and I wanted to dress in English fashion so Karl went shopping for me and bought me different clothes and outfits and a coat. Everything fit me perfectly. I didn't know how he managed to get the right size.*

"*Karl rented a room a mile or so away. He looked after the* grounds surrounding the big house for 1 or 2 days each week so I was able to see him occasionally. On Thursdays my day was free and we were able to meet and go to the cinema and then to dinner. Sometimes we would take the train to London to the theatre.

"Although my employer was good to me it was a difficult time as everything was so different. I didn't know anyone or anything about England. I thought should I go home? I wasn't even sure Karl was going to marry me."

"After a year I decided to leave the job as I saw an advertisement for another position in the area that promised me 10 shillings more, giving me £2 a week so I took the job. My new employers were a Baron and Baroness. I had lodgings in their big house and helped with their two small children. The Baroness also had a daughter from her first marriage. Her name was Mary. She was 17 years old and was very shy. The family had two dogs and Mary would walk them and feed them. Her mother wanted her to learn to dance so they sent her to a dance school in London. I went with her as her escort. She also had to learn to curtsy to the Queen as she was preparing to be presented as a debutante.

"Around this time, I received news in a letter from my sister that my dear Papa had died. He had gone back home to my mother. He was 54 years old. He had spent so many years in hospital. He became ill and wrote me one last letter from the hospital in Branice.

"On 30th March 1951 we were married at Woking Registry Office. The Baron and Baroness were very nice to us. They were our witnesses and they drove us to the wedding in their Rolls Royce and provided a small reception for us after the wedding ceremony.

"In the summer of 1951 we visited the Festival of Britain in London and we went to the (newly built) Festival Hall near Waterloo. One day we visited Battersea Gardens as there was a carnival. We spent the whole day there. There was a boating pond with gondolas and a carousel. There was so much to see.
Yes, it was a wonderful time for us.

"The Baron spoke several languages and also owned a Chateau in the South of France. Each autumn the whole family *would travel to the warmer weather of the South of France and spend 6 months at the Chateau. They asked Karl and I to go with them for the season but we didn't want to go as we had travelled enough. We just wanted to be settled and so we looked around for somewhere else to live and work.*

"There was a family in Weybridge who owned a nice big house that had a three-room first floor apartment to rent. The wife was French and both the husband and the wife's mothers lived in the house too. Karl worked in the garden and I worked in the kitchen. Most of the meals included rice! The husband worked for a bank and they had lived in Hong Kong for many years. Some Sundays they would have garden parties and invite colleagues from London. The garden had to look spick and span and they served lots of food and drink to their guests. There was also a girl from France, Deniese, who helped out. It was everything we could have dreamed of. Karl and I were very happy."

When Hildegard found she was expecting her first child, she and Karl decided they needed a home of their own, their first independent home being a boat on the River Bourne. In September 1952 Hildegard gave birth to a son, Karl, who they named after his father. When the boat sprang a leak Karl Snr found a new job with a small house included in Chertsey. One year later, in September 1953, twins Karin and Susan were born, with Diana making the family complete in March 1958. Around this time the family were granted a larger house, also in Chertsey, where Hildegard still lives at the time of writing.

Although Hildegard loved her new life in England, she missed her mother and sister very much and she carried a sense of guilt over many years knowing she had deserted them at such a difficult time. Thanks to many letters to and from her mother and her sister they were able to stay closely in touch, until 1961 when her mother sadly died aged 59.

Gretel and Erich eventually moved to Frankfurt and regular contact by post continued with Gretel. Eventually the telephone gave the sisters the opportunity to speak to each other each week. Hildegard and Karl also managed a few trips to visit Gretel and Erich in Frankfurt, including some with their children, and enjoyed time spent in the couple's Schrebergarten.

Hildegard continued to feel guilty for leaving Gretel who had suffered so much since her departure. Erich was a jolly man and loved socialising and dancing. He had come from a long line of farmers and before their wedding his mother asked him "Why are you marrying Gretel? She isn't from a farming family!" Hearing of this, Gretel did all she could to impress her strict and humourless mother-in-law. She would rise at 5am each day to feed the cows and clean the barn, but it was hard work and she wasn't strong. She soon found she was expecting a baby. She was so happy. Hildegard remembered how Gretel's job at the kindergarten had given her such a love for children that parents would often ask her to babysit. She would sometimes invite the children to their home in Jaginne and she would see how happy her sister was when surrounded by children, playing with them and teaching them songs and rhymes. However, as Gretel felt compelled to continue with the heavy chores to please her mother-in-law, the devastating effect was the sad loss of her much longed for baby. When she heard the news Hildegard wished she could go and help her sister. Poor Gretel. She so desperately wanted a child of her own. With the added problem that hospitals in Poland in those days were not very well equipped, Gretel received little to no help, support or advice, culminating in the loss of two more babies and the inability to conceive more. Hildegard could only send her love from afar but was glad that in the following years she could introduce her own children to her sister who became an interested though distant Tante.

As Hildegard and Karl settled into family life in England, Gretel heard that a woman in a nearby village to hers had a sister who had also moved to England and she had recently returned to visit her family. The woman told her that her sister had married an Englishman and they were now living in Guildford in Surrey. Gretel realised this might be quite near to Chertsey and asked for her telephone number which she passed to Hildegard. The sister's name was Gertrude and she was married to Bert. Hildegard telephoned her and Gertrude said "Please come over and see us. I still have sausage from Poland!" She and Karl visited the couple and thus began a friendship that spanned many years. It was so good for both women to have a friend from their homeland.

Another German lady, Ruth, also lived in Chertsey and became a good friend of Karl and Hildegard. Ruth had been a Red Cross nurse in Breslau (now Wroclaw) and was there during the time of the siege. She had been allowed to stay in the East due to her nursing skills but later married an Englishman and came to live in England.

When the children were very young Hildegard also found kindness and encouragement in her friendship with two local English ladies, Ruby and Ivy. She was so grateful to them for the help and support they gave her as a mother of four young children with no extended family to assist.

As the children grew it was coincidental that two of Karin and Susan's friends had German mothers, one named Honey and the other Inge. The three ladies met through their daughters but became lifelong friends and enjoyed many happy times together, sharing their lives. More often than not they conversed with each other in German which was so natural and beneficial to each of them as they celebrated their common heritage.

Despite being in a foreign land without parents or her sister or anyone she knew from her country of birth, Hildegard, from the moment she set foot on British soil, had been blessed by much kindness and wonderful new friendships. She also joined the Catholic community at St Anne's Church in Chertsey which she regularly attended over many years and made many friends.

Chapter 50

Faith, Hope and Love

Hildegard's young life involved many twists and turns. After a carefree childhood, the end of the war brought her into many difficult and fearful situations, causing her to take risks and make life changing decisions whilst experiencing loss and uncertainty, grief and sadness. Her faith helped her find the courage she didn't realise she possessed and when faced with problems she prayed and trusted God. She prayed for the protection of herself, her family and her friends and was able to cope with every challenge with tenacity and positivity, ultimately being grateful to have been saved from undue peril.

Hildegard found a good man in Karl and for years held on to her hope of a future with him, leading her to the decision to leave her family and her homeland to be with the man she loved. They finally found peace and safety together in England where they happily settled down and created a family. Sadly, her beloved Karl died suddenly and prematurely from a heart attack in 1984 at the age of 65. Hildegard was heartbroken. But in time, instead of being beaten by this huge loss in her life, at the age of 60 she took up new and sociable hobbies such as country dancing and rambling and she joined the local and vibrant 'Monday Club' taking part in various activities including trips abroad for holidays. She was determined to continue to live her life to the full.

Unfortunately, a fall resulting in a broken ankle in her mid-90s called a halt to Hildegard's active social life and she became housebound, eventually being advised to remain in bed. Thankfully a hospital bed was set up downstairs in the hub of her own home with very helpful and kind carers calling in four times a day to care for all her physical needs.

As Hildegard could no longer attend church, the church came to her. The local priest and members of the congregation continue to visit her and bring Communion as well as friendship and prayers. Although physically unable to look after herself in her later years, Hildegard's mind thankfully remains sound and her amazing memory still sharp. She effortlessly recited the Lord's Prayer on her 101st birthday when her church brought her Communion.

Thanks to excellent and expert support, Hildegard continues to enjoy the love and care of her 4 children and their families. She has been blessed with 6 grandchildren and, at the time of going to print in 2025, 7 great grandchildren.

A life well lived.

Postscript

The expulsion of *Volksdeutsche* from the east: Was it a wise decision? Was it fair and humane?

With the motive being to avoid further wars, the Allied Powers proposed and agreed the idea that each affected European country should comprise only those of that country's ethnicity. Due to the moving of borders over the centuries, millions of ethnic Germans had made homes in neighbouring countries and tensions between Germans and non-Germans had been a recurring problem.

A quote from Winston Churchill in 1945: "Expulsion is the method which, as far as we have seen, will be the most satisfactory and lasting. There will be no mixture of populations to cause endless trouble."

With the redrawing of borders towards the end of WWII, a third of German land, mainly that along the eastern territories, was being granted to neighbouring countries such as Czechoslovakia and Poland.

The expulsion of all *Volksdeutsche* (ethnic Germans) from their homes along the length of East Germany, east of the River Oder, as well as those living in East European countries, created the largest movement or transfer of any population in modern European history.

Although records vary it is thought that, between 1944-1948, 12-14million Germans had fled or been expelled from Germany's eastern territories and East European countries, 7million of them were from the areas newly annexed to Poland. Estimated deaths relating to the expulsions ranged from 500,000 to 2.5million.

Russia's Red Army, whose occupation of the eastern territories had already begun, was called upon to assist and supervise the expulsions. When Churchill received news of gross mistreatment of expellees, he issued a directive for the task to be carried out in an "orderly and humane fashion". Soviets however, considering all Germans to be part of the Nazi regime that reneged on an agreement and attacked their country killing millions, ignored the instruction.

Those who escaped the clutches of the Red Army on the perilous journey west were extremely fortunate as many who were apprehended, especially women, faced untold horrors. Also at this time, ethnic Germans living further into Eastern Europe, young and old, were being forced out of their homes and sent to work camps in Russia to endure the most brutal conditions and treatment. The inescapable and despicable atrocities that many had to suffer is indescribable. Innocent German civilians forced to pay for Adolf Hitler's sins.

Robert Murphy, political adviser to General Eisenhower, one of the Allied Powers responsible for the expulsions, voiced his criticism of the plan, saying "The mind reverts to other mass deportations which horrified the world and brought upon the Nazis the odium which they so deserved. Those (previous) mass deportations engineered by the Nazis provided part of the moral basis on which we waged war and which gave strength to our cause. Now the situation is reversed we find ourselves in the invidious position of being partners in this German enterprise and as partners inevitably sharing the responsibility." The American government thence tried hard to reverse the rulings, but to no avail.

The sad results of the expulsions included family members lost and never found. Many never able to return to the place they and generations before them had lived and worked and brought up their families. Homes and property which had been handed down through the years, never to be returned to their rightful owners. Thousands of deaths and millions of misplaced persons/refugees. Years on, such expulsions would be deemed illegal under international law, eg the Geneva Convention or the European Human Rights Convention.

The fate of expellees had no means of improving as there were no treaties and no refugee aid to help them. Their rights and the return of ancestral homes are still uncertain to this day. Expulsion and the ensuing horrors reshaped expellees' lives forever.

Bund der Vertriebenen (The Federation of Expellees) was set up in the 1950s. Its belief was that "the right to the homeland is recognised and carried out as one of the fundamental rights of mankind given by God"; with the added requirement to renounce all revenge and retaliation. Over the years, organisations such as this have helped expellees to reclaim their homes and land.

BIBLIOGRAPHY

Military Wiki
BBC Bitesize
History of Sorts
Warsaw Institute
National WWII Museum
Wikipedia
AnneFrank.org
Orderly and Humane by RM Douglas
Encyclopaedia Britannica
Holocaust Encyclopaedia
GCSE History by Clever Lili
British Library
The House by the Lake by Thomas Harding
Six Minutes in May by Nicholas Shakespeare
Google Maps
Quora
History Hustle
Over Simplified
The Second Holocaust by T Emerson May
Forgotten Voices by Ulrich Merten
US Holocaust Memorial Museum
Infocentra Mesta, Karlovy Vary
Encyclopaedia of Alabama
Map Wikimedia Commons, photo and licensed under the Creative Commons Attribution-Share Alike 2.5 Generic license